FLORENCE NIGHTINGALE

A BIOGRAPHY

BY

ANNIE MATHESON

AUTHOR OF

"THE STORY OF A BRAVE CHILD (JOAN OF ARC)"

THOMAS NELSON AND SONS, LTD.

LONDON, EDINBURGH, AND NEW YORK

First published in

1913

LONDON, NEW YORK,

Florence Nightingale.

(From a model of the statue by A. G. Walker.   By kind permission of the Sculptor.)

"The Lady with the Lamp."

(From the statuette in the Nightingale Home.)

PREFACE.

IT is hardly necessary to say that this little biography is based mainly upon the work of others,
though I hope and believe it is honest enough to
have an individuality of its own and it has certainly cost endless individual labour and anxiety.
Few tasks in literature are in practice more
worrying than the responsibility of " piecing
together " other people's fragments, and " the
great unknown " who in reviewing my " Leaves
of Prose " thought I had found an easy way
of turning myself into respectable cement for
a tessellated pavement made of other people's
chipped marble, was evidently a stranger to my
particular temperament. Where I have been
free to express myself without regard to others,
to use only my own language, and utter only my
own views, I have had something of the feeling
of a child out for a holiday, and of course the
greater part of the book is in my own words.
But I have often, for obvious reasons, chosen the
humbler task, because, wherever it is possible, it

is good that my readers should have their impressions at first hand, and in regard to Kinglake especially, from whose non-copyright volumes I have given many a page, his masculine tribute to Miss Nightingale is of infinitely more value than any words which could come from me.

My publisher has kindly allowed me to leave many questions of copyright to him, but I wish, not the less—rather the more—to thank all those authors and publishers who have permitted use of their material and whose names will, in many instances, be found incorporated in the text or in the accompanying footnotes. I have not thought it necessary in every instance to give a reference to volume and page, though occasionally, for some special reason of my own, I have done so.

Of those in closest touch with Miss Nightingale during her lifetime, whose help with original material has been invaluable, not more than one can be thanked by name. But to Mrs. Tooley for her large-hearted generosity with regard to her own admirable biography—to which I owe far more than the mere quotations so kindly permitted, and in most cases so clearly acknowledged in the text—it is a great pleasure to express my thanksgiving publicly.

There are many others who have helped me, and not once with regard to the little sketch have I met with any unkindness or rebuff. Indeed, so various are the acknowledgments due, and so sincere the gratitude I feel, that I scarcely know where to begin.

To Miss Rickards, for the pages from her beautiful life of Felicia Skene, I wish to record heartfelt thanks ; and also to Messrs. Burns and Oates with regard to lengthy quotations from the letters of Sister Aloysius—a deeply interesting little volume published by them in 1904, under the title of "A Sister of Mercy's Memories of the Crimea ; " to Dr. Hagberg Wright of the London Library for the prolonged loan of a whole library of books of reference and the help always accessible to his subscribers ; and to the librarian of the Derby Free Library for aid in verifying pedigree. Also to Lord Stanmore for his generous permission to use long extracts from his father's " Life of Lord Herbert," from which more than one valuable letter has been taken ; and to Mr. John Murray for sanctioning this and for like privileges in relation to the lives of Sir John MacNeill and Sir Bartle Frere. To Messrs. William Blackwood, Messrs. Cassell, Messrs. G. P. Putnam and Sons, as well as to the editors and publishers of the *Times*, *Daily Telegraph*, *Morning Post*, and *Evening News*, I wish to add my thanks to those of my publisher.

To any reader of this book it will be clear how great a debt I owe to General Evatt, and he knows, I think, how sincerely I recognize it. Mr. Stephen Paget, the writer of the article on Miss Nightingale in the Dictionary of National Biography, has not only permitted me to quote from that—a privilege for which I must also thank Messrs. Smith Elder, and Sir Sidney Lee—but has, in addition, put me in the way of other priceless material wherewith to do honour to the subject of this biography. I have long been grateful to him for the inspiration and charm of his own "Confessio Medici"—there is now this other obligation to add to that.

Nor can I forgo cordial acknowledgments to the writer and also the publisher of the charming sketch of Miss Nightingale's Life published some years ago by the Pilgrim Press and entitled "The Story of Florence Nightingale."

To my friend Dr. Lewis N. Chase I owe the rare privilege of an introduction to Mr. Walker, the sculptor, who has so graciously permitted for my frontispiece a reproduction of the statue he has just completed as a part of our national memorial to Miss Nightingale.

I desire to thank Miss Rosalind Paget for directing me to sources of information and bestowing on me treasures of time and of memory, as well as Miss Eleanor F. Rathbone and the writer of Sir John MacNeill's Life for help given by their books, and Miss Marion Holmes for permission to quote from her inspiring monograph ; and last, but by no means least, to express my sense of the self-sacrificing magnanimity with which Miss E. Brierly, the present editor of *Nursing Notes*, at once offered me and placed in my hands—what I should never have dreamed of asking, even had I been a friend of old standing, instead of a comparative stranger—everything she herself had gathered together and preserved as bearing on the life of Florence Nightingale.

When, under the influence of certain articles in the *Times*, I undertook to write this volume for Messrs. Nelson, I knew nothing of the other biographies in the field. Nor had I any idea that an officially authorized life was about to be written by Sir Edward Cook, a biographer with an intellectual equipment far beyond my own, but who will not perhaps grudge me the name of friend, since his courteous considerateness for all leads many others to make a like claim, and the knowledge that he would put no obstacle in my path has spared me what might have been a serious difficulty. Had I known all this, a decent modesty might have prevented my undertaking. But in every direction unforeseen help has been showered upon me, and nothing but my own inexorable limitations have stood in my way.

If there be any who, by their books, or in any other way, have helped me, but whom by some unhappy oversight I have omitted to name in these brief documentary thanks, I must earnestly beg them to believe that such an error is contrary to my intention and goodwill.

CONTENTS

LIST OF ILLUSTRATIONS

INTRODUCTORY CHAPTER FOR THE ELDERS IN MY AUDIENCE.

IT is my hope that my younger readers may find this volume all the more to their liking if it is not without interest to people of my own generation. Girls and boys of fourteen to sixteen are already on the threshold of manhood and womanhood, but even of children I am sure it is true that they hate to be "written down to," since they are eagerly drinking in hopes and ideas which they cannot always put into words, and to such hopes and ideas they give eager sympathy of heart and curiosity of mind.

For one of her St. Thomas's nurses, among the first nine women to be decorated with the Red Cross, the heroine of this story wrote what might well be the marching orders of many a good soldier in the divine army, and not least, perhaps, of those boy scouts and girl guides who would like better a life of adventure than the discipline of a big school or the "duties enough and little cares" of a luxurious home ; and as the words have not, so far as I am aware, appeared in print before, it may be worth while to give them here :—

"Soldiers," she wrote, "must obey orders. And to you the 'roughing' it has been the resigning yourself to 'comforts' which you detested and to work which you did not want, while the work which wanted you was within reach. A severe kind of 'roughing' indeed—perhaps the severest, as I know by sad experience.

"But it will not last. This short war is not life. But all will depend—your possible future in the work, we pray for you, O my Cape of Good Hope—upon the name you gain here. That name I know will be of one who obeys authority, however unreasonable, in the name of Him who is above all, and who is Reason itself—of one who submits to disagreeables, how-

(1,764)

Florence Nightingale's Home, Embley Park, Romsey, Hants.

ever unjust, for the work's sake and for His who tells us to love those we don't like—a precept I follow oh so badly—of one who never criticizes so that it can even be guessed at that she has criticism in her heart—and who helps her companions to submit by her own noble example. . . .

"I have sometimes found in my life that the very hindrances I had been deploring were there expressly to fit me for the next step in my life. (This was the case—hindrances of *years*—before the Crimean War.)" And elsewhere she writes: "To have secured for you all the *circumstances* we wished for your work, I would gladly have given my life. But you are made to rise above circumstances; perhaps this is God's way—His ways are not as our ways—of preparing you for the great work which I am persuaded He has in store for you some day."

It is touching to find her adding in parenthesis that before her own work was given to her by the Great Unseen Commander, she had ten years of contradictions and disappointments, and adding, as if with a sigh from the heart, " And oh, how badly I did it!"

There we have the humility of true greatness. All her work was amazing in its fruitfulness, but those who knew her best feel sometimes that the part of her work which was greatest of all and will endure longest is just the part of which most people know least. I mean her great labour of love for India, which I cannot doubt has already saved the lives of millions, and will in the future save the health and working power of millions more.

Florence Nightingale would have enriched our calendar of uncanonized saints even if her disciplined high-hearted goodness had exercised an unseen spell by simply *being*, and had, by some limitation of body or of circumstance, been cut off from much active *doing*: for so loving and obedient a human will, looking ever to the Highest, as a handmaiden watches the eyes of her mistress, is always and everywhere a humane influence and a divine offering. But in her life—a light set on a hill—being and doing went hand in hand in twofold beauty and strength, for even through those years when she lay on her bed, a secluded prisoner, her activities were world-wide.

In addition to the work for which she is most widely revered and loved, Miss Nightingale did three things—each leaving a golden imprint upon the history of our time :—

She broke down a "Chinese wall" of prejudice with regard to the occupations of women, and opened up a new and delightful sphere of hard, but congenial, work for girls.

She helped to reconstruct, on the lines of feminine common sense, the hygiene and the transport service of our army—yes, of the entire imperial army, for what is a success in one branch of our dominions cannot permanently remain unaccepted by the rest. And in all her work for our army she had, up to the time of his death, unbounded help from her friend, Lord Herbert.

Last, and perhaps greatest of all, she initiated, with the help of Sir Bartle Frere, Sir John Lawrence, and other enlightened men of her time, the reform of insanitary and death-dealing neglect throughout the length and breadth of India, thus saving countless lives, not only from death, but from what is far worse—a maimed or invalid existence of lowered vitality and lessened mental powers.

One of her friends, himself a great army doctor holding a high official position, has repeatedly spoken of her to me as the supreme embodiment of citizenship. She did indeed exemplify what Ruskin so nobly expressed in his essay on " Queens' Gardens "—the fact that, while men and women differ profoundly and essentially, and life would lose in beauty if they did not, the state has need of them both; for what the woman should be at her own hearth, the guardian of order, of health, of beauty, and of love, that also should she be at that wider imperial hearth where there are children to be educated, soldiers to be equipped, wounded lives to be tended, and the health of this and future generations to be diligently guarded.

" Think," she said once to one of her nurses, " less of what you may gain than of what you

may give." Herself, she gave royally—gave her
fortune, her life, her soul's treasure. I read in
a recent contemporary of high standing a
review which ended with what seemed to me
a very heathen sentence, which stamped itself
on my memory by its arrogant narrowness.
"Woman," wrote the reviewer, "is always
either frustrate or absorbed;" and there leaped
to my heart the exclamation, "Here in Florence
Nightingale is the answer; for in her we have
one, known and read of all men, who was
neither the one nor the other." That there
was supreme renunciation in her life, none
who is born to womanhood can doubt; for
where could there be any who would have
been more superbly fitted for what she herself regarded as the natural lot of woman
as wife and mother? But she, brilliant,
beautiful, and worshipped, was called to a
more difficult and lonely path, and if there
was hidden suffering, it did but make her
service of mankind the more untiring, her
practical and keen-edged intellect the more
active in good work, her tenderness to pain

and humility of self-effacement the more beautiful and just.

It has been said, and said truly, that she did not suffer fools gladly, and she knew well how very human she was in this and in other ways, as far removed from a cold and statuesque faultlessness as are all ardent, swift, loving natures here on earth. But her words were words of wisdom when she wrote to one dear to her whom she playfully named "her Cape of Good Hope": "Let us be persecuted for righteousness' sake, *but not for unrighteousness.*"

The italics are mine, because in their warning they seem so singularly timely. And the entire sentence is completely in tune with that fine note with which she ends one of her delightful volumes on nursing—

"I would earnestly ask my sisters to keep clear of both the jargons now current everywhere (for they are equally jargons): of the jargon, namely, about the 'rights' of women which· urges women to do all that men do, including the medical and other professions,

merely because men do it, and without regard
to whether this *is* the best that women can
do; and of the jargon which urges women to
do nothing that men do, merely because they
are women, and should be 'recalled to a sense
of their duty as women,' and because 'this
is women's work,' and 'that is men's,' and
'these are things which women should not
do,' which is all assertion and nothing more.
Surely woman should bring the best she has,
whatever that is, to the work of God's world,
without attending to either of these cries.
For what are they, both of them, the one
just as much as the other, but listening to the
'what people will say,' to opinion, to the
'voices from without'? And as a wise man
has said, no one has ever done anything great or
useful by listening to the voices from without.

"You do not want the effect of your good
things to be, 'How wonderful for a *woman!*'
nor would you be deterred from good things
by hearing it said, 'Yes, but she ought not
to have done this, because it is not suitable
for a woman.' But you want to do the thing

that is good, whether it is 'suitable for a woman,' or not.

"It does not make a thing good, that it is remarkable that a woman should have been able to do it. Neither does it make a thing bad, which would have been good had a man done it, that it has been done by a woman.

"Oh, leave these jargons, and go your way straight to God's work, in simplicity and singleness of heart."

CHAPTER I.

IN the heart of Derbyshire there is a quaint old church, once a private chapel, and possessing, instead of a churchyard, a bit of quiet greenness, of which the chief ornament, besides the old yew tree at the church door, is a kind of lovers' bower made by two ancient elder trees which have so intertwined their branches as to form an arbour, where in summer-time sweethearts can gossip and the children play. It belonged to a world far away from the world of to-day, when, in the high-backed pews reserved for the "quality," little Florence Nightingale, in her Sunday attire that was completed by Leghorn hat and sandal shoes, made, Sunday after Sunday, a pretty vision for the villagers, in whose cottages she was early a welcome visitor. It was just such a church as we read of in George Eliot's stories, clerk and parson dividing the service between them, and the rustic bareness of the stone walls matched by the visible bell-ropes and the benches for the labouring people. But the special story that has come down from those days suggests that the parson was more satirical than Mr. Gilfil or Mr. Tryan, and it is to be feared that when he remarked that "a lie is a very useful thing in trade," the people who quoted him in Derby market-place merely used his "Devil's text" as a convenience and saw no satire in it at all. Have we really travelled a little way towards honesty since those days, or have we grown more hypocritical?

The little girl in the squire's pew grew up in a home where religious shams were not likely to be taken at their face value.

Her father, who was one of the chief supporters of the cheap schools of the neighbourhood, had his own ways of helping the poor folk on his estate, but used to reply to some of the beseeching people who wanted money from him for local charities that he was "not born generous." Generous or not, he had very decided views about the education of his two children, Florence and Parthe. They enjoyed nearly a hundred years ago (Florence was born in 1820) as liberal a course of study as any High School girl of to-day, and no doubt it is true that the orderliness of mind and character, at which his methods aimed, proved of countless value to Florence in those later days, when her marvellous power in providing for minutest details without unnecessary fuss or friction banished the filth and chaos of the first Crimean hospitals, and transformed them into abodes of healing and of order. She grew up to be a beautiful and charming woman, for whom men would gladly have laid down their lives; yet her beauty and her charm alone could not have secured for our wounded soldiers in the Crimea, tortured by dirt and neglect, the swift change to cleanness and comfort and good nursing which her masterly and unbending methods aided her commanding personal influence to win.

But this is leaping too far ahead. As yet she is only Parthenope's little playfellow and school-fellow in the room devoted to " lessons " at Lea

Hall, the small maiden who climbs the hill on Sundays to the church where the yew tree guards the door, and on week-days is busy or at play in the house that has been the home of her father's family through many generations, and in the grounds of the manor that surround it.

Lea Hall is in that part of the country which Father Benson has described in his novel, "Come Rack, come Rope," and the Nightingale children were within easy reach of Dethick Hall, where young Anthony Babington had lived. It must have added zest to their history lessons and their girlish romancings to hear of the secret passage, which was supposed to lead right into Wingfield Manor, from the underground cellar close to the old wall that showed still where Dethick had once reared its stately buildings. The fact that the farm bailiff now kept his potatoes there and could not find the opening, would only make it a constant new ground for adventure and imagination. For they would be told of course —these children—how Mary Stuart had once been a prisoner at Dethick, and Anthony had vowed to be her servant in life or death and

never cease from the struggle to set her free
so long as life was in him.   Nor did he; for
he died before her, and it was not at Wingfield, but at Fotheringay, as these little
students very well knew, no doubt, that her
lovely head soon afterwards was laid upon the
block.

Enviable children to have such a playground
of imagination at their doors!   But, indeed, all
children have that, and a bare room in a slum,
or a little patch of desert ground, may for them
be danced over by Queen Mab and all her fairies,
or guarded by the very angel who led St. Peter
out of prison.   Still, it is very exciting to have
history written beside the doorstep where you
live, and if you grow up in a home where lesson
books are an important part of the day's duties,
it is pleasant to find them making adventures for
you on your father's own estate.   It mattered
nothing that the story would all be told by those
contending against Anthony's particular form of
religion, who would be ready to paint him with
as black an ink as their regard for justice would
allow.   To a child, that would rather enhance

the vividness of it all. And there was the actual kitchen still standing, with its little harmless-looking trapdoor in the roof that leads into the secret chamber, where the persecuted priests used to hide when they came to celebrate a secret Mass. No wonder the two children delighted in Dethick, and wove many a tale about it. For had they not seen with their very own eyes the great open fireplace in that kitchen, where venison used to be roasted, and the very roasting-jack hanging from its central beam where all the roof-beams were black with age and dark with many tragic memories?

Dethick is but one of the three villages included in the ancient manor, the other two are Lea and Holloway; and in the days of King John, long before it came to the Nightingales, the De Alveleys had built a chapel there. Those who have read Mr. Skipton's life of Nicholas Ferrar and know their John Inglesant, will be interested to hear that half this manor had passed through the hands of the Ferrars among others, and another portion had belonged to families whose names suggest a French origin. But the two inheritances had now met in the hands of the Nightingales.

It is a very enchanting part of the Midlands. The silvery Derwent winds through the valleys, keeping fresh the fields of buttercups and meadow-sweet and clover, and in the tall hedges wild roses mingle their sweetness with the more power-ful fragrance of the honeysuckle, until both yield to the strange and overwhelming perfume of the elder tree. The limestone hills, with their bold and mountainlike outline, their tiny rills, and exquisite ferns, had been less spoiled in those days by the tramp of tourists; and the purity of the air, the peacefulness of the upland solitudes, would have a wholesome share in the "grace that can mould the maiden's form by silent sympathy."

It was a very youthful little maiden as yet who had been transplanted into these English wilds from the glory and the sunshine of the Italy where she was born. After the valley of the Arno and the splendours of Florence, it may have seemed somewhat cold and bracing at times. Rightly or wrongly, the father of the little girls

—for our heroine's sister, named after another Italian city, shared all her life at this time— seems to a mere outsider a little cold and bracing too. He came of a very old family, and we hear of his "pride of birth." His wife, on the other hand, whom Florence Nightingale resembled, lives before us in more warm and glowing colours, as one who did much to break down the barriers of caste and, with a heart of overflowing love, "went about doing good." Both were people of real cultivation—good breeding being theirs by a happy inheritance—and each seems to have had a strong and distinctive personality. It might not be easy to say to which of the two the little daughter, who grew to such world-wide fame, owed most; but probably the equipment for her life-work was fairly divided between the two. There is no magnet so powerful as force of character, and it is clear that her father possessed moral and intellectual force of a notable sort. Love, in the sense of enthusiasm for humanity, will always be the heaven-born gift of one in whom religion is such a reality as it was with Florence Nightingale,

Florence Nightingale's Father.

but religious ardour may be sadly ineffective if defeated by the slack habits of a lifetime, or even by a moral and mental vagueness that befogs holy intentions. Mr. Edward Nightingale's daughters were disciplined in a schoolroom where slackness and disorder were not permitted, and a somewhat severe training in the classics was supplemented by the example of Mrs. Nightingale's excellent housewifery, and by that fine self-control in manners and behaviour which in the old-fashioned days used to be named " deportment." Sports and outdoor exercises were a part—and a delightful part—of the day's routine.

But let us go back a few years and give a few pages to the place of Florence Nightingale's birth and the history of her family. Her name, like that of another social reformer among Englishwomen, was linked with Italy, and she took it from the famous old Italian town in whose neighbourhood she was born. I have tried in vain to trace the authorship *—was it Ruskin or

* I wrote to the author of the charming sketch of Florence Nightingale in which I found it quoted, but he has quite forgotten who was the writer.

some less known writer ?—who said of that town,
"if you wish to see it to perfection, fix upon
such a day as Florence owes the sun, and, climb-
ing the hill of Bellosguardo, or past the stages of
the Via Crucis to the church of San Miniato,
look forth upon the scene before you. You
trace the course of the Arno from the distant
mountains on the right, through the heart of the
city, winding along the fruitful valley toward
Pisa. The city is beneath you, like a pearl set
in emerald. All colours are in the landscape,
and all sounds are in the air. The hills look
almost heathery. The sombre olive and funereal
cypress blend with the graceful acacia and the
clasping vine. The hum of the insect and the
carol of bird chime with the blithe voices of
men; while dome, tower, mountains, the yellow
river, the quaint bridges, spires, palaces, gardens,
and the cloudless heavens overhanging, make up
a panorama on which to gaze in trance of rapture
until the spirit wearies from the exceeding beauty
of the vision."

When on May 12, 1820, Florence Nightingale was born, her parents were staying at the

Villa Colombaia, near to this beautiful City of
Flowers; and when the question of a name for
her arose, they were of one mind about it—she
must be called after the city itself.   They had no
sons, and this child's elder sister, their only other
daughter, having been born at Naples, had taken
its ancient and classical name of Parthenope.*

Their own family name had changed.   Mr.
Nightingale, who was first known as William
Edward Shore, was the only son of Mr. William
Shore of Tapton, in Derbyshire, and the child
who was to reform England's benighted views
of nursing, and do so much for the health, not
only of our British troops, but also of our Indian
Army, was related through that family to John
Shore, a famous physician in Derby in the reign
of Charles the Second, as well as to the Governor-
General of India who, twenty-three years before
her birth, took the title of Baron Teignmouth.
It was through her father's mother, the only
daughter of Mr. Evans of Cromford, that she
was linked with the family of the Nightingales,
whose name her father afterwards took.   Mary

* Her full name was Frances Parthenope Nightingale.

Evans, her paternal grandmother, was the niece of " Old Peter," a rich and roystering squire, who was well liked in his own neighbourhood, in spite of his nickname of " Madman Peter " and the rages that now and then overtook him. Florence Nightingale was, however, no descendant of his, for he never married, and all his possessions, except those which he sold to Sir Richard Arkwright, the famous cotton-spinner, came to his niece, who was the mother of Miss Nightingale's father. When all this landed property came into the hands of Mr. Edward Shore, three years before his marriage and five years before Florence was born, his name was changed under the Prince Regent's sign manual from Shore to Nightingale, in accordance with Peter Nightingale's will. But he continued to live in Italy for a great part of every year until Florence was nearly five years old, though the change of ownership on the English estate was at once felt under the new squire, who was in most ways the very opposite of that " Old Peter," of whom we read that when he had been drinking, as was then the fashion, he would frighten away the servant-maids by rushing into the kitchen and throwing the puddings on the dust-heap.

Mr. Edward Nightingale, our heroine's father, bore a character without fear or reproach. Educated at Edinburgh and at Trinity, Cambridge, he had afterwards travelled a good deal, at a time when travel was by no means the commonplace that it is now.

He is described as " tall and slim," and from the descriptions we have of him it is clear that no one, even at a glance, could have missed the note of distinction in his bearing, or mistaken him for other than that which he was proud to be, the cultivated and enlightened son of a fine old family.

When we read that the lady he married was daughter of a strong Abolitionist, Mr. William Smith of Parndon, in Essex, we feel that the very name of Abolitionist belongs to a bygone past.

In those days the American Civil War was still to come, but the horizon was already beginning to blacken for it, just as in Europe, while two happy little girls were playing hide-and-seek in the gardens of Lea Hall and racing with their

dogs across the meadows to Dethick, the hush
before the tempest did not blind wise statesmen
to those dangers in the Near East which were to
overwhelm us in so terrible a war.

Mr. Smith, in desiring ardently the abolition
of slavery, was ahead of many Englishmen of his
day. He was an eager philanthropist, who for
half a century represented Norwich in Parliament,
and had therefore real power in urging any good
cause he had at heart. His daughter Frances,
when she became Mrs. Nightingale, did not cease
to labour among the poor in the spirit of her
father and of her own benevolent heart. She
was a beautiful and impressive woman, and in
her untiring service of others seems to have been
just the wife for Mr. Nightingale, who was ready
to further every good work in his own neighbourhood. He, in his artistic and scholarly
tastes, was as humane and enlightened as was the
woman of his choice in her own skill of hand
and charm of household guidance.

For Mrs. Nightingale was not only a notable
housekeeper and her husband's companion in the
world of books, she was also a woman whose

individuality of thought and action had been deepened by her practical faith, so that even at a time when England was still tied and bound by conventions of rank, from which the last fifty years have released many devotees, she felt the call of the Master to a deeper and wider sense of brotherhood, and had a great wish to break through artificial barriers.

As a matter of fact, she found many innocent ways of doing so. But she did not know in these early days that in giving to the world a little daughter who was akin to her in this, she had found the best way of all; for that daughter was to serve others in the very spirit of those great ones of old—S. Teresa and S. Catharine and the Blessed Joan of Arc—to whom the real things were so real and so continually present that the world's voices were as nothing in comparison. This was true also of Mrs. Browning, whose memory has already come to mind, as linked, like that of Florence Nightingale, though for quite other reasons, with the City of Flowers; and although a life of action in the ordinary sense was impossible for the author of "Aurora Leigh," yet it is remarkable how much she also did to arouse and set free her sisters, for she too, like the others, was a woman of great practical discernment.

The little peasant maid of France, who was born to be a warrior and the deliverer of her people, had this in common with the little English girl born to a great inheritance and aiming at a higher and humbler estate wherein she was the queen of nurses, that both cared so much for the commands from above as to be very little influenced by the gossip round about.

CHAPTER II.

FLORENCE was between five and six years old when the Nightingales moved from Lea Hall into their new home at Lea Hurst, a house commanding a specially beautiful outlook, and built under Mr. Nightingale's own supervision with much care and taste, about a mile from the old home. It is only fourteen miles out of Derby, though there would seem to be many sleepy inhabitants of that aristocratic old town—like the old lady of Hendon who lived on into the twentieth century without having been into the roaring city of London hard by—who know nothing of the attractions within a few miles of them ; for Mrs. Tooley tells an amusing story of a photographer there who supposed Lea Hurst to be a distinguished man and a local celebrity.

To some it seemed that there was a certain

bleakness in the country surrounding Lea Hall, but, though the two dwellings are so short a distance apart, Lea Hurst is set in a far more perfect landscape. Hills and woodlands, stretching far away to Dovedale, are commanded by the broad terrace of upland on which the house stands, and it looks across to the bold escarpment known as Crich Stand, while deep below, the Derwent makes music on its rocky course. Among the foxglove and the bracken, the gritstone rocks jutting forth are a hovering place for butterflies and a haunt of the wild bee.

The house itself—shaped like a cross, gabled and mullioned, and heightened by substantial chimney-stacks—is solid, unpretending, satisfying to the eye. Above the fine oriel window in the drawing-room wing is the balcony pointed out to visitors where, they are told, after the Crimea "Miss Florence used to come out and speak to the people."

The building of the house was completed in 1825, and above the door that date is inscribed, together with the letter N. The drawing-room

and library look south, and open on to the
garden, and "from the library a flight of stone
steps leads down to the lawn." In the centre
of the garden front an old chapel has been built
into the mansion, and it may be that the prayers
of the unknown dead have been answered in the
life of the child who grew up under its shadow,
and to whom the busy toiling world has owed
so much.

The terraced garden at the back of the house,
with its sweet old-fashioned flowers and blossoming apple trees, has doubtless grown more delightful with every year of its advancing age, but what
an interest the two little girls must have had
when it was first being planted out and each could
find a home for her favourite flowers! Fuchsias
were among those loved by little Florence, who,
as has already been noted, was only six years old
when she and her sister and father and mother
moved into Lea Hurst, and there was a large
bed of these outside the chapel. The old schoolroom and nursery at the back of the house look
out upon the hills, and in a quiet corner of the
garden there is a summer-house where Florence

and her only sister, who had no brothers to share their games, must often have played and worked.

Lea Hurst is a quiet, beautiful home, characteristically English and unpretending, with a modest park-gate, and beyond the park those Lea Woods where the hyacinths bloom and where it is still told how "Miss Florence" loved to walk through the long winding avenue with its grand views of the distant hills and woods.

But the Nightingales did not spend the whole year at Lea Hurst. In the autumn it was their custom to move to Embley, in Hampshire, where they spent the winter and early spring. They usually sent the servants on ahead with the luggage, and drove by easy stages in their own carriage, taking the journey at leisure, and putting up at inns by the way. Sometimes, of course, they travelled by coach. Those of us who only know the Derby road in the neighbourhood of towns like Nottingham and Derby now that its coaching glories are past, find it difficult to picture its gaiety in those old coaching days, when the very horses enjoyed the liveliness of the running, and the many carriages with their

gay postilions and varied occupants were on the
alert for neighbour or friend who might be post-
ing in the same direction.

Whether in autumn or in spring, the drive
must have been a joy. The varied beauty of
the Midlands recalls the lines in " Aurora Leigh "
which speak of

> " Such nooks of valleys lined with orchises,
>   Fed full of noises by invisible streams ;
>   And open pastures where you scarcely tell
>   White daisies from white dew,   .   .   .
>   .   .   . the clouds, the fields,
>   The happy violets hiding from the roads
>   The primroses run down to, carrying gold ;
>   The tangled hedgerows, where the cows push out
>   Impatient horns and tolerant churning mouths
>   'Twixt dripping ash-boughs,—hedgerows all alive
>   With birds and gnats and large white butterflies
>   Which look as if the May-flower had caught life
>   And palpitated forth upon the wind ;
>   Hills, vales, woods, netted in a silver mist,
>   Farms, granges, doubled up among the hills;
>   And cattle grazing in the watered vales,
>   And cottage-chimneys smoking from the woods,
>   And cottage-gardens smelling everywhere,
>   Confused with smell of orchards."

Derbyshire itself, with its wild lilies of the
valley, its ferns and daffodils and laughing
streams, is hardly more " taking " than the

country through which winds the silver Trent,
past Nottingham Castle, perched on its rock and
promontory above the fields where the wild
crocus in those days made sheets of vivid purple,
and the steep banks of Clifton Grove, with its
shoals of blue forget-me-not, making a dim, tree-
crowned outline, with here and there a gleam of
silver, as seen by the chariots " on the road."
Wollaton Park, with its great beeches and limes
and glimpses of shy deer, would give gold and
crimson and a thousand shades of russet to the
picture.

And farther south, at the other end of the
journey, what miles of orchards and pine woods
and sweet-scented heather—what rolling Downs
and Surrey homesteads along the turnpike roads !

Though Parthenope and Florence had no
brothers to play with them, they seem to have
had a great variety of active occupations, both
at Lea Hurst and at Embley. Of course they
had their dolls, like other little girls ; but those
which belonged to Florence had a way of falling
into the doctor's hands—an imaginary doctor, of
course—and needing a good deal of tender care

and attention. Florence seemed never tired of
looking after their various ailments. In fact,
she had at times a whole dolls' hospital to tend.
She probably picked up a little amateur knowledge of medicine quite early in life ; for the
poor people in the neighbourhood used to come
to her mother for help in any little emergency,
and Mrs. Nightingale was, like many another
Lady Bountiful of her generation, equipped with
a certain amount of traditional wisdom and kindly
common sense, aided in her case by wider reading
and a better educated mind than the ordinary.

Florence, having somehow escaped measles
and whooping-cough, was not allowed to run
into infection in the cottages, but that did not
prevent the sending of beef-teas and jellies and
other helpful and neighbourly gifts, which
could be tied to her pony's saddle-bow and
left by her at the door. She learned to know
the cottagers with a frank and very human
intimacy, and their homely wit touched her
own, their shrewdness and sympathy met their
like in her, and as she grew older, all this
added to her power and her charm. She

learned to know both the north and the south in "her ain countree," and when, later in life, she was the wise angel of hope to the brave "Tommies," recruited from such homes, meeting them as she did amid unrecorded agonies that were far worse than the horrors of the battlefield, she understood them all the better as men, because she had known just such boys as they had been and was familiar with just such homes as those in which they grew up. According to Mrs. Tooley's biography, the farmhouse where Adam Bede fell in love with Hetty was just the other side of the meadows at Lea Hurst, and the old mill-wheel, where Maggie Tulliver's father ground the corn of the neighbourhood, was only two or three miles away. Marian Evans, of whom the world still thinks and speaks by her pen-name of George Eliot, came sometimes to visit her kinsfolk in the thatched cottage by Wirksworth Tape Mills, and has left us in her earlier novels a vivid picture of the cottage life that surrounded our heroine during that part of the year which she spent in the

Derbyshire home. The children, of course, had their own garden, which they dug and watered, and Florence was so fond of flowers and animals that that again was an added bond with her rustic neighbours. Flower-missions had not in those days been heard of, but she often tied up a nosegay of wild flowers for invalid villagers, or took some of her favourites out of her own garden to the sick people whom she visited.

The story of her first patient has already been told several times in print, but no biography would be complete without it.

She had nursed many dolls back to convalescence—to say nothing of " setting " their broken limbs—tempted their delicate appetites with dainties offered on toy plates, and dressed the burns when her sister let them tumble too near the nursery fire ; but as yet she had had no real human patient, when one day, out riding with her friend the vicar over the Hampshire Downs near Embley, they noticed that Roger, an old shepherd whom they knew very well, was having endless trouble in getting his sheep together.

"Where's Cap?" asked the vicar, drawing up his horse, for Cap was a very capable and trusted sheep-dog.

"'T' boys have been throwing stones at 'n and they've broken t' poor chap's leg. Won't ever be any good no more, a'm thinkin'. Best put him out of 's misery."

"O Roger!" exclaimed a clear young voice, "poor Cap's leg broken? Can't we do anything for him?"

"Where is he?" added Florence eagerly, for the voice was that of the future "Queen of Nurses." "Oh, we can't leave him all alone in his pain. Just think how cruel!"

"Us can't do no good, miss, nor you nayther. I'se just take a cord to him to-night; 'tis the only way to ease his pain."

But Florence turned to plead with the vicar, and to beg that some further effort should be made.

The vicar, urged by the compassion in the young face looking up to his, turned his horse's head in the right direction for a visit to Cap. In a moment Florence's pony was put to the gallop, and she was the first to arrive at the shed where the poor dog was lying.

Cap's faithful brown eyes were soon lifted to hers, as she tenderly tried to make him understand her loving sympathy, caressing him with her little hand and speaking soothingly with her own lips and eyes; till, like the suffering men whose wounds would in the far-off years be eased through her skill, the dog looked up at her in dumb and worshipping gratitude.

The vicar was equal to the occasion, and soon discovered that the leg was not broken at all, but badly bruised and swollen, and perhaps an even greater source of danger and pain than if there had merely been a broken bone.

When he suggested a "compress," his child-companion was puzzled for a moment. She thought she knew all about poultices and bandages, and I daresay she had often given her dolls a mustard plaster; but a "compress" sounded like something new and mysterious. It was, of course, a great relief when she learned that she only needed to keep soaking cloths in hot water, wringing them out, and folding them over Cap's injured leg, renewing them as quickly as they cooled. She was a nimble little person, and, with the help of the shepherd boy, soon got a fire of sticks kindled in a neighbouring cottage and the kettle singing on it with the necessary boiling water. But now what to do for cloths? Time is of importance in sick-nursing when every moment of delay means added pain to the sufferer. To ride home would have meant the loss of an hour or two, and thrifty cottagers are not always ready to tear up scant and cherished house-linen for the nursing of dogs. But Florence was not to be baffled. To her great delight she espied the shepherd's smock hanging up behind the door. She was a fearless soul, and felt no doubt whatever that her mother would pay for a new smock. "This will just do," she said, and, since that delightful vicar gave a nod of entire approval, she promptly tore it into strips.

Then back to Cap's hut she hastened, with her small henchman beside her carrying the kettle and the basin; for by this time he, the boy shepherd, began to be interested too, and the vicar's superintendence was no longer needed. A message of explanation was sent to Embley that Mr. and Mrs. Nightingale might not be anxious, and for several hours Florence gave herself up to nursing her patient. Cap was passive in her hands, and the hot fomentations gradually lessened the pain and the swelling.

Imagine the wonder and gratitude of old Roger when he turned up with the rope in his hand and a leaden weight on his poor old heart! Cap, of course, knew his step and greeted him with a little whine of satisfaction, as if to be the first to tell him the good news.

"Why, missy, you have been doing wonders," he said. "I never thought to see t' poor dog look up at me like that again."

"Yes," exclaimed the happy young nurse; "doesn't he look better? Well, Roger, you can throw away the rope. I shall want you to help me make these hot compresses."

"Miss Florence is quite right, Roger," interposed the vicar; "you'll soon have Cap running about again."

"I'm sure I cannot thank you and the young lady enough, yer riv'rence. And I'll mind all the instrooctions for he."

As the faithful dog looked up at him, eased and content, it was a very happy man that was old Roger. But the doctor-nurse was not prepared to lose her occupation too quickly.

"I shall come and see him again to-morrow, Roger," she said; "I know mamma will let me, when I just explain to her about it all."

CHAPTER III.

The weaving of many threads, both of evil and of good.

WHILE Florence Nightingale and her sister were working hard at history and languages and all useful feminine arts, romping in the sunny Hampshire gardens, or riding amongst the Derbyshire hills, the big world outside their quiet paradise was heaping fuel for the fires of war, which at last, when after a quarter of a century it flared up out of its long-prepared combustibles, was " to bring to death a million workmen and soldiers, consume vast wealth, shatter the framework of the European system, and make it hard henceforth for any nation to be safe except by sheer strength." And above all its devastation, remembered as a part of its undying record, the name of one of these happy children was to be blazoned on the page of history.

Already at the beginning of the century the first Napoleon had said that the Czar of Russia was always threatening Constantinople and never taking it, and by the time Florence Nightingale was twelve years old, it might be said of that Czar that while "holding the boundless authority of an Oriental potentate," his power was supplemented by the far-reaching transmission of his orders across the telegraph wires, and if Kinglake does not exaggerate, "he would touch the bell and kindle a war, without hearing counsel from any living man."

The project against Constantinople was a scheme of conquest continually to be delayed, but never discarded, and, happen what might, it was never to be endured that the prospect of Russia's attaining some day to the Bosphorus should be shut out by the ambition of any other Power. Nicholas was quite aware that multitudes of the pious throughout his vast dominions dwelt upon the thought of their co-religionists under the Turkish rule, and looked to the shining cross of St. Sophia, symbol of their faith above the church founded by Constantine, as the goal of political unity for a "suppliant nation."

And Kinglake tells us with an almost acid irony of Louis Napoleon, that he who was by the Senatus-Consulte of 1804 the statutory heir of the great Bonaparte, and after his exile and imprisonment had returned to France, laboured to show all men "how beautifully Nature in her infinite wisdom had adapted that same France to the service of the Bonapartes ; and how, without the fostering care of these same Bonapartes, the creature was doomed to degenerate, and to perish out of the world, and was considering how it was possible at the beginning of the nineteenth century to make the coarse Bonaparte yoke of 1804 sit kindly upon her neck."

The day was drawing near when a great war would seem to him to offer just the opportunity he wanted.

Far away as yet was that awful massacre of peaceful citizens in Paris in 1851, with which the name of Louis Napoleon was associated as responsible for the *coup d'état* — a massacre probably the result of brutal panic on the part of the soldiers, the civilians, and that craven president, Louis Napoleon himself, whose conscience made a coward of him, and whose terror usually took the form of brutality—but long before that date, by his callous plotting and underhand self-seeking, he was preparing forces which then made for death and terror, and by that time had more or less broken the manhood of his beautiful Paris.

Yet all over the world at all times, while the enemy is sowing tares in the field, the good seed is ripening also in the ground for the harvest; and through these same years faroff threads were being woven, ready to make part of the warp and woof of a life, as yet busied with the duties and joys of childhood, but one day to thrill the hearts of Europe and be remembered while time shall last.

Elizabeth Fry, who was to be one of its decisive influences, was bringing new light and hope into the noisome prisons of a bygone century, and we shall see how her life-work was not without its influence later on the life of the child growing up at Embley and Lea Hurst.

And a child nearly of Florence Nightingale's own age, who was one day to cross her path with friendly help at an important crisis, was playing with her sister Curlinda—Sir Walter Scott's nickname for her real name of Caroline —and being drilled in manners in French schools in Paris and Versailles, before her family moved to Edinburgh and her more serious lessons began. This was Felicia Skene, who was afterwards able to give momentary, but highly important help, at a critical moment in Florence Nightingale's career. Like Florence herself, she was born amid romantic surroundings, though not in Italy but in Provence, and was named after her French godmother, a certain Comtesse de Felicité. Her two earliest recollections were of the alarming and enraged gesticulations of Liszt when giving a music lesson to her frightened sisters, and the very different vision of a lumbering coach and six accompanied by mounted soldiers—the coach and six wherein sat Charles the Tenth, who was soon afterwards to take refuge in Holyrood. That was in Paris, where her family went to live when she was six years old, but at the time of Cap's accident they had already moved to Edinburgh, where her chief friends and playmates were the little Lockharts and the children of the murdered Duc de Berri. It was there that Sir Walter Scott, on the day when he heard of his bankruptcy, came and sat quietly by the little Felicia, and bade her tell him fairy stories, as he didn't want to talk much himself. He was an old and dear friend of her father, one link between them being the fact that Mr. Skene was related by marriage to the beautiful Williamina Stuart with whom Scott in his early days had fallen deeply and ardently in love.

The little Felicia was at this time a very lively child and full of innocent mischief. Her later devotion to the sick and poor did not begin so early as was the case with Florence Nightingale, though there came a time when she and Florence met in after life as equals and fellow-soldiers in the great campaign against human suffering. Her travels and adventures in Greece and her popularity at the Athenian court were

still hidden in the future, and while Florence at
Embley and Lea Hurst was gradually unfolding
a sweetness of nature that was by no means blind
to the humorous side of things, and a highly
practical thoroughness in all she undertook,
Felicia was enjoying a merry home-life under the
governorship of Miss Palmer, whom she nick-
named Pompey, and being prepared for confirma-
tion by her father's friend, Dean Ramsay. We
are told of her that she might have said with
Coppée, " J'ai eu toujours besoin de Dieu." Full
of fun and of interest in life's great adventure,
for others quite as much as for herself, religion
was the moving force that moulded the soul
of her to much unforeseen self-sacrifice as yet
undreamed.

CHAPTER IV.

The activities of girlhood—Elizabeth Fry—Felicia Skene again.

BUT we are wandering away from Embley and from the two daughters of the squire, who were already the delight of the village.

Cap was by no means the only animal who owed much to Florence, and Peggy, a favourite old pony, now holiday-making in the paddock, looked for frequent visits and much sport between lesson hours.

" Poor old Peggy, then ; would she like a carrot ? "

" Well, where is it, then ?   See if you can find it, Peggy."

And then a little game followed, to which the beloved pony was quite accustomed—snuffing round her young mistress and being teased and tantalized for a minute or two, just to heighten the coming pleasure, until at last the pocket was found where the precious delicacy was hidden, and the daily feast began, a feast not of carrots only, for caresses were of course a part of the ritual.

Florence had much good fellowship also with the wild squirrels of the neighbourhood, especially in one long avenue that was their favourite abode. They were not in the least afraid of her, and would come leaping down after the nuts that she dropped for them as she walked along. Sometimes she would turn sharp round and startle them back into their homes, but it was easy to tempt them down again. She was quick at finding and guarding the nests of brooding birds, and suffered very keenly as a child when the young ones were taken away from their mothers.

Lambs and calves soon learned that she was fond of them, and the affection was not on her side only. But among the pets that the two girls were allowed to have, the ailing ones were always the most interesting to the future nurse.

It cannot, however, be too strongly stated that there was nothing sentimental or lackadaisical in the very vigorous and hard-working life that she

led.   It was not by any means all songs and roses,
though it was full of the happiness of a well-
ordered and loving existence.   Her father was
a rigid disciplinarian, and nothing casual or easy-
going was allowed in the Embley schoolroom.
For any work carelessly done there was punishment as well as reproof, and no shamming of any
sort was allowed.   Hours must be punctually
kept, and, whether the lesson for the moment
was Latin, Greek, or mathematics, or the sewing
of a fine and exquisite seam, it must come up to
the necessary standard and be satisfactorily done.
The master-mind that so swiftly transformed the
filthy horrors of Scutari into a well-ordered hospital, and could dare to walk through minor
difficulties and objections as though they did not
exist, was educated in a severe and early school;
and the striking modesty and gentleness of Florence Nightingale's girlhood was the deeper for
having grappled with enough real knowledge to
know its own ignorances and limitations, and
treat the personality of others with a deference
which was a part of her charm.

And if study was made a serious business, the

sisters enjoyed to the full the healthy advantages of country life.   They scampered about the park with their dogs, rode their ponies over hill and dale, spent long days in the woods among the bluebells and primroses, and in summer tumbled about in the sweet-scented hay.   "During the summer at Lea Hurst, lessons were a little relaxed in favour of outdoor life ; but on the return to Embley for the winter, schoolroom routine was again enforced on very strict lines." *

In Florence Nightingale's Derbyshire home the experiments in methods of healing which dispensed with drugs could not fail to arouse attention and discussion, for Mr. John Smedley's newly-built cure-house stood at the foot of the hill below Lea Hurst, and before Florence Nightingale was twenty she had already begun to turn her attention definitely in the direction of nursing.   Everything tended to deepen this idea. She was already able to do much for the villagers, and in any case of illness they were always eager to let her know.   The consumptive girl whose room she gladdened with flowers was but one of

* Mrs. Tooley, p. 37.

the many ailing folk who found comfort and joy in her presence. "Miss Florence had a way with her that made them feel better," they said.

In those days nursing as a profession did not exist. When it was not done wholly for love by the unselfish maiden aunt or sister, who was supposed, as a matter of course, to be always at the disposal of the sick people among her kinsfolk, it had come to be too often a mere callous trade, carried on by ignorant and grasping women, who were not even clean or of good character. The turning of a Scutari hell into a hospital that seemed heaven by comparison, was a smaller miracle than that which Miss Nightingale's influence was destined later to achieve in changing a despised and brutalized occupation throughout a whole empire into a noble and distinguished art.

Of course it must never be forgotten that through all the centuries since the Christian Church was founded, there had been Catholic sisterhoods with whom the real and the ideal were one—Sisters of Mercy, who were not only refined and cultivated gentlewomen, but the most devoted and self-sacrificing of human souls.

And now in England, in that Society of Friends, which among Christian communities might seem outwardly farthest away from a communion valuing as its very language the ancient symbols and ritual of the Catholic Church, yet was perhaps by its obedience to the inward voice more in sympathy with the sisterhoods of that Church than were many other religious groups, there had been lifted up by Elizabeth Fry a new standard of duty in this matter, which in her hands became a new standard of nursing, to be passed on in old age by her saintly hands into the young and powerful grasp of the brilliant girl who is the heroine of our story. The name of Elizabeth Fry is associated with the reform of our prisons, but it is less commonly known that she was also a pioneer of decent nursing. She understood with entire simplicity the words, " I was sick and in prison, and ye visited me." Perhaps it was not mere coincidence that the words occur in the " lesson " appointed for the 15th of February— the day noted in Elizabeth Fry's journal as the date of that visit to Newgate, when the poor felons she was yearning to help fell on their knees and prayed to a divine unseen Presence. In a recent number of the *Times* which celebrates her centenary a quotation from her diary is given which tells in her own words :—

"I heard weeping, and I thought they appeared much tendered ; a very solemn quiet was observed ; it was a striking scene, the poor people on their knees around us, in their deplorable condition."

And the *Times* goes on to say, " nothing appears but those qualities of helpfulness, sympathy, and love which could tame the most savage natures, silence the voice of profanity and blasphemy, and subdue all around her by a sense of her common sisterhood even with the vilest of them in the love of God and the service of man. . . . But the deepest note of her nature was an intense enthusiasm of humanity. It was this which inspired and sustained all her efforts from first to last—even in her earlier and more frivolous days—for the welfare and uplifting of

her fellow-creatures ; and it is only right to add
that it was itself sustained by her deep and
abiding conviction that it is only by the love
of God that the service of man can be sanctified
and made to prosper." A letter followed next
day from Mr. Julian Hill, who actually remem-
bers her, and tells how the Institution of Nursing
Sisters which she organized grew out of her deep
pity for the victims of Sairey Gamp and her
kind.

All this was preparing the way for the wider
and more successful nursing crusade in which
her memory and influence were to inspire the
brave young soul of Florence Nightingale.
Speaking of all the difficulties that a blindly
conventional world is always ready to throw in
the way of any such new path, her old friend
writes : " Such difficulties Mrs. Fry and Miss
Nightingale brushed contemptuously aside."

But in our story Miss Nightingale is as yet
only lately out of the schoolroom. And Elizabeth Fry's life was by no means alone, as we
have seen, in its preparation of her appointed
path, for about the time that Florence Nightin-

gale was taking her place in the brilliant society that met about her father's board, and Felicia Skene was " coming out," a new experiment was being made by a devout member of the Lutheran Church, an experiment which was to play an important part in the world's history, though so quietly and unobtrusively carried out.

We must not anticipate—we shall read of that in a later chapter.

CHAPTER V.

Home duties and pleasures—The brewing of war.

FLORENCE was very happy as her mother's almoner, and in her modest and unobtrusive way was the life and soul of the village festivities that centred in the church and school and were planned in many instances by her father and mother. It is one of the happy characteristics of our time that much innocent grace and merriment have been revived in the teaching of beautiful old morris dances and other peasant festivities that had been banished by the rigour of a perverted Puritanism, and the squire of Lea Hurst and his wife were before their time in such matters. There was a yearly function of prize-giving and speech-making and dancing, known as the children's " Feast Day," to which the scholars came in procession to the Hall, with their wreaths and garlands, to the music of a good marching band provided by the squire, and afterwards they had tea in the fields below the Hall garden, served by Mrs. Nightingale and her daughters and the Hall servants, and then ended their day with merry outdoor dancing. For the little ones Florence planned all kinds of games; the children, indeed, were her special care, and by the time the evening sun was making pomp of gold and purple in the sky above the valley of the Derwent, there came the crowning event of the day when on the garden terrace the two daughters of the house distributed their gifts to the happy scholars.

Mrs. Tooley in her biography calls up for us in a line or two a vision of Florence as she was remembered by one old lady, who had often been present and recalled her slender charm, herself as sweet as the rose which she often wore in her neatly braided hair, brown hair with a glint of gold in it, glossy and smooth and characteristic of youth and health. We have from one and another a glimpse of the harmonious simplicity also of her dress—the soft muslin gown, the little silk fichu crossed

upon her breast, the modest Leghorn bonnet
with its rose. Or in winter, riding about in
the neighbourhood of Embley and distributing
her little personal gifts at Christmas among
the old women—tea and warm petticoats—her
" ermine tippet and muff and beaver hat."

She helped in the training of young voices
in the village, and was among the entertainers
when the carol-singers enjoyed their mince-pies
and annual coins in the hall. The workhouse
knew her well, and any wise enterprise in the
neighbourhood for help or healing among the
poor and the sad was sure of her presence and of
all the co-operation in the power of her neighbours, Mr. and Mrs. Sidney Herbert, with whom
for some years before the Crimea she shared
much companionship in such work. This
friendship was an important influence in our
heroine's life, for Mr. Herbert was of those
who reveal to the dullest a little of the divine
beauty and love, and his wife was through all
their married life his faithful and devoted friend,
so that they made a strong trio of sympathetic
workers ; for " Liz," as her husband usually

called her in his letters to their common friend
Florence Nightingale, seemed to have fully shared
his unbounded faith in the noble powers and high
aims of the said Florence, whom she too loved
and admired.   She was a daughter of General
Charles Ashe à Court, and she and Sidney
Herbert had known one another as children.
Indeed, it was in those early days, when she
was quite a little child, that Elizabeth, who
grew up to be one of the most beautiful women
of her day, said of Sidney, then, of course, a mere
boy, that that was the boy she was going to
marry, and that she would never marry any one
else.   Many a long year, however, had rolled
between before he rode over to Amington from
Drayton, where he often met her, though no
longer such near neighbours as in the early
Wiltshire days, and asked the beautiful Elizabeth
to be his wife.   The intimacy between the two
families had never ceased, and General à Court,
himself member for Wilton, had worked hard
for Sidney's first election for the county.   We
shall hear more of these dear and early friends
of Florence Nightingale as her story un-

folds, but let us turn now for a moment to herself.

Her life was many-sided, and her devotion to good works did not arise from any lack of knowledge of the world. She was presented, of course, like other girls of her order, and had her "seasons" in London as well as her share in country society. A young and lovely girl, whose father had been wise enough to give her all the education and advantages of a promising boy, and who excelled also in every distinctive feminine accomplishment and "pure womanliness," had her earthly kingdom at her feet. But her soul was more and more deeply bent on a life spent in service and consecrated to the good of others. Her Sunday class, in the old building known as the "Chapel" at Lea Hurst, was but one of her many efforts in her father's special domain in Derbyshire, and girls of every faith came to her there without distinction of creed. They were mostly workers in the hosiery mills owned by John Smedley, and many of them, like their master, were Methodists. She sang to them, and they still remember the sweetness of her voice and " how beautifully Miss Florence used to talk," as they sat together through many a sunny afternoon in the tiny stone building overlooking Lea Hurst gardens. Cromford Church, built by Sir Richard Arkwright, was then comparatively new, and time had not made of it the pretty picture that it is now, in its bosoming trees above the river ; but it played a considerable part in Florence Nightingale's youth, when the vicar and the Arkwright of her day—old Sir Richard's tomb in the chancel bears the earlier date of 1792—organized many a kind scheme for the good of the parish, in which the squire's two daughters gave their help.

But Miss Nightingale was not of a type to consider these amateur pleasures a sufficient training for her life-work, and that life-work was already taking a more or less definite shape in her mind.

She herself has written :—

" I would say to all young ladies who are called to any particular vocation, qualify yourselves for it as a man does for his work.   Don't think you can undertake it otherwise.   Submit yourselves to the rules of business as men do, by which alone you can make God's business succeed, for He has never said that He will give His success and His blessing to sketchy and unfinished work."   And on another occasion she wrote that " three-fourths of the whole mischief in women's lives arises from their excepting themselves from the rules of training considered needful for men."

It has already been said that her thought was more and more directed towards nursing, and in various ways she was quietly preparing herself to that end.

Her interview with the Quaker-saint, Elizabeth Fry, though deliberately sought and of abiding effect, was but a brief episode.   It was about this time that they met in London.   The serene old Quakeress, through whose countenance looked forth such a heavenly soul, was no doubt keenly interested in the ardent, witty, beautiful girl who came to her for inspiration and counsel.

They had much in common, and who knows but the older woman, with all her weight of experience, her saintly character, and ripened harvest, may yet in some ways have felt herself the younger of the two ; for she had come to that quiet threshold of the life beyond, where a soul like hers has part in the simple joys of the Divine Child, and looks tenderly on those who are still in the fires of battle through which they have passed.

Her own girlhood had defied in innocent ways the strictness of the Quaker rule.   Imagine a young Quakeress of those days wearing, as she had done on occasion, a red riding habit !

She had been fond of dancing, and would have, I suspect, a very healthy human interest in the activities of a girl in Society, though she would enter into Florence Nightingale's resolve that her life should not be frittered away in a self-centred round, while men and women, for whom her Master died, were themselves suffering a slow death in workhouses and prisons and hospitals, with none to tend their wounds of soul and body.

Be this as it may—and without a record of their conversation it is easy to go astray in imagining—we do know that like all the greatest saints they were both very practical in their Christianity, and did not care too much what was thought of their actions, so long as they were right in the sight of God. In their common sense, their humility, their warm, quick-beating heart of humanity, they were kindred spirits.

The interview bore fruit even outwardly afterwards in a very important way. For it was from Elizabeth Fry that Florence Nightingale first heard of Pastor Fliedner and his institute for training nurses at Kaiserswerth, as well as of Elizabeth Fry's own institute for a like purpose in London, which first suggested the Kaiserswerth training home, thus returning in ever-widening blessing the harvest of its seed.

Her desire was for definite preparatory knowledge and discipline, and we of this generation can hardly realize how much searching must have been necessary before the adequate training could be found. Certificated nursing is now a commonplace, and we forget that it dates from Miss Nightingale's efforts after her return from the Crimea. We have only to turn to the life of Felicia Skene and her lonely labour of love at the time when the cholera visited Oxford—some twelve years later than Florence Nightingale's seventeenth birthday, that is to say, in 1849–51, and again in 1854—to gain some idea of the bareness of the field. Sir Henry Acland, whose intimate friendship with Felicia dates from their common labours among the cholera patients, has described one among the terrible cases for which there would, it seems, have been no human aid, but for their discovery of the patient's neglected helplessness.

"She had no blanket," he says, "or any covering but the ragged cotton clothes she had on. She rolled screaming. One woman, scarcely sober, sat by; she sat with a pipe in her mouth, looking on. To treat her in this state was hopeless. She was to be removed. There was a press of work at the hospital, and a delay. When the carriers came, her saturated garments were stripped off, and in the finer linen and in the blankets of a wealthier woman she was borne away, and in the hospital she died."

This is given, it would seem, as but one case among hundreds.

Three old cattle-sheds were turned into a sort of impromptu hospital, to which some of the smallpox and cholera patients were carried, and the clergy, especially Mr. Charles Marriott and Mr. Venables, did all they could for old and young alike, seconding the doctors, with Sir Henry at their head, in cheering and helping every one in the stricken town ; and Miss Skene's friend, Miss Hughes, Sister Marion, directed the women called in to help, who there received a kind of rough-and-ready training. But more overwhelming still was Miss Skene's own work of home nursing in the cottages, at first single-handed, and afterwards at the head of a band of women engaged by the deputy chairman as her servants in the work, of whom many were ignorant and needed training. " By day and by night she visited," writes Sir Henry.

"She plied this task, and when she rested—or where as long at least as she knew of a house where disease had entered—is known to herself alone."

Meanwhile a critical moment had arisen in the affairs of Europe. Our own Premier, Lord Aberdeen, had long been regarded as the very head and front of the Peace Movement in England, and when he succeeded the wary Lord Palmerston, it is said that Nicholas, the Czar of Russia, made no secret of his pleasure in the event, for he saw tokens in England of what might at least leave him a chance of pulling Turkey to pieces. He seems also to have had a great personal liking for our ambassador, Sir Hamilton Seymour, who was fortunately a man of honour as well as a man of discretion and ready wit. The account given by Kinglake of the conversations in which the Emperor Nicholas disclosed his views, and was not permitted to hint them merely, makes very dramatic reading. The Czar persisted in speaking of Turkey as a very sick man, whose affairs had better be taken out of his hands by his friends before his final dissolution. Sir Hamilton courteously intimated that England did not treat her allies in that manner; but Nicholas was not to be put off, and at a party given by the Grand Duchess Hereditary on February 20, 1853, he again took Sir Hamilton apart, and in a very gracious and confidential manner closed his conversation with the words, "I repeat to you that the sick man is dying, and we can never allow such an event to take us by surprise. We must come to some understanding."

The next day he explained how the partition should in his opinion be made. Servia and Bulgaria should be independent states under his protection. England should have Egypt and Candia. He had already made it clear that he should expect us to pledge ourselves not to occupy Constantinople, though he could not himself give us a like undertaking.

"As I did not wish," writes Sir Hamilton Seymour, "that the Emperor should imagine that an English public servant was caught by this sort of overture, I simply answered that I had always understood that the English views upon

Egypt did not go beyond the point of securing a safe and ready communication between British India and the mother country. 'Well,' said the Emperor, 'induce your Government to write again upon these subjects, to write more fully, and to do so without hesitation. I have confidence in the English Government. It is not an engagement, a convention, which I ask of them; it is a free interchange of ideas, and in case of need the word of a "gentleman"—that is enough between us.'"

In reply, our Government disclaimed all idea of aiming at any of the Sultan's possessions, or considering the Ottoman Empire ready to fall to bits; and while accepting the Emperor's word that he would not himself grab any part of it, refused most decisively to enter on any secret understanding.

All through 1853 these parleyings were kept secret, and in the meantime the Czar had failed in his rôle of tempter. In the interval the Sultan, who perhaps had gained some inkling of what was going on, suddenly yielded to Austria's demand that he should withdraw certain troops that had been harassing Montenegro, and thereby rousing the Czar's religious zeal on behalf of his co-religionists in that province. Everything for the moment lulled his previous intention of a war against Turkey.

But the Emperor Louis Napoleon had in cold blood been driving a wedge into the peace of the world by reviving a treaty of 1740, which had given to Latin monks a key to the chief door of the Church of Bethlehem, as well as the keys to the two doors of the Sacred Manger, and also the right to place a silver star adorned with the arms of France in the Sanctuary of the Nativity. That the Churches should fight for the key to the supposed birthplace of the Prince of Peace is indeed grotesque. But the old temple had in His day become a den of thieves; and even the new temple, built through His own loving sacrifice, is ever being put to uses that are childish and greedy.

It is not difficult to understand that, by means of this treaty, awakening the vanity and greed that cloak themselves under more decent feelings in such rivalries, Louis Napoleon made his profit for the moment out of the powers of evil.

The Czar's jealousy for his own empire's Greek version of the faith made the triumph of this treaty wormwood to him and to his people. "To the indignation," Count Nesselrode writes, " of the whole people following the Greek ritual, the key of the Church of Bethlehem has been made over to the Latins, so as publicly to demonstrate their religious supremacy in the East." . . .

" A crowd of monks with bare foreheads," says Kinglake, " stood quarrelling for a key at the sunny gates of a church in Palestine, but beyond and above, towering high in the misty North, men saw the ambition of the Czars."

The Czars did not stand alone: " some fifty millions of men in Russia held one creed, and they held it too with the earnestness of which Western Europe used to have experience in earlier times. . . . They knew that in the Turkish dominions there were ten or fourteen millions of men holding exactly the same faith as themselves . . . they had heard tales of the sufferings of these their brethren which seemed," they blindly thought, " to call for vengeance."

Nicholas himself was a fanatic on such questions, and the end of it was that his rage hoodwinked his conscience, and he stole a march upon England and France, which destroyed their trust in his honour. He had already gathered troops in the south, to say nothing of a fleet in the Euxine ; and having determined on an embassy to Constantinople, he chose Mentschikoff as his messenger, a man who was said to hate the Turks and dislike the English, and who, according to Kinglake, was a wit rather than a diplomat or a soldier. Advancing with much of the pomp of war, and disregarding much of the etiquette of peace, his arrival and behaviour caused such a panic in the Turkish capital that Colonel Rose was besought to take an English fleet to the protection of the Ottoman Empire. Colonel Rose's friendly willingness, though afterwards cancelled by our Home Government, at once quieted the terror in Constantinople ; but the Emperor of the French cast oil upon the smouldering flame by sending a fleet to Salamis. This greatly angered Nicholas, and, although he was pleased to find England disapproved of what France had done, Mentschikoff offered a secret treaty to Turkey, with ships and men, if she ever needed help, and asked in return for complete control of the Greek Church. This broke all his promises to the Western Powers, and England at once was made aware of it by the Turkish minister.

Prince Mentschikoff meanwhile drew to himself an army, and the English Vice-consul at Galatz reported that in Bessarabia preparations were already made for the passage of 120,000 men, while battalions from all directions were making southward—the fleet was even then at Sebastopol.

The double-dealing of Russia was met by a gradual and tacit alliance between England and the Sultan; and Lord Aberdeen, whose love of peace has been described by one historian as "passionate" and "fanatical," was unknowingly tying his own hands by the advice he gave in his

Florence Nightingale.

(From the painting in the National Portrait Gallery by Augustus Egg, R.A.)

despatches when consulted by Turkey. Moreover, in Turkey, our ambassador, Lord Stratford de Redcliffe, stiffened the back of Ottoman resistance against the Czar's wily handling of "the sick man." Lord Stratford's tact and force of character had moulded all to his will, and our admiral at Malta was told to obey any directions he received from him. Our fleets were ordered into the neighbourhood of the Dardanelles, and Lord Stratford held his watch at Therapia against the gathering wrath of the Czar. Only a very little kindling touch was needed to light the fires of a terrible conflict in Europe.

CHAPTER VI.

Pastor Fliedner.

A PEBBLE thrown into a lake sends the tiny circ-
ling ripples very far, and one good piece of work
leads to others of a quite different kind. Pastor
Fliedner, inspired by love to his Master and
deeply interested in Elizabeth Fry's efforts, began
to help prisoners. Finding no nurses for those
of them who were ill, he was led to found the
institution at Kaiserswerth, where Miss Nightingale afterwards received a part of her training.

His story is a beautiful one. His father and
grandfather had both been pastors in the Lutheran
Church, and, like so many sons of the Manse, he
was exceedingly poor, but he lived to justify his
name of Theodor. He was born twenty years
before Miss Nightingale, in the village of Epp-
stein, and perhaps he was the more determined
to prove to himself and others that he had a

soul, because he was one of those plump children
who get teased for looking like dumplings, and
when his father laughingly called him the " little
beer-brewer " he didn't like it, for he was a
bit thin-skinned.   He worked his way bravely
through school and college, Giessen and Göt-
tingen, and not only earned his fees by teaching,
but also his bread and roof ; and when teaching
was not enough, he had the good sense to turn
shoeblack and carpenter and odd man.   He
valued all that opens the eyes of the mind and
educates what is highest and best.   Many a
time, heedless of hardship and privation, he
would, in his holidays, tramp long distances that
he might see more of God's world and learn
more of men and things.   He taught himself
in this way to speak several languages, learned
the useful healing properties of many herbs, and
other homely knowledge that afterwards helped
him in his work among the sick.   Then, too,
the games and songs that he picked up on his
travels afterwards enriched his own kindergarten.
While tutoring at Cologne, he did quite informally
some of the work of a curate, and, through preach-

ing sometimes in the prison, became interested in the lot of discharged prisoners. It was at Cologne too that he received from the mother of his pupils kindly suggestions as to his own manners, which led him to write what is as true as it is quaint, that " gentle ways and polite manners help greatly to further the Kingdom of God."

He was only twenty-two when he became pastor of the little Protestant flock at Kaiserswerth, having walked there on foot and purposely taken his parishioners by surprise that they might not be put to the expense of a formal welcome. His yearly salary was only twenty pounds, and he helped his widowed mother by sharing the parsonage with a sister and two younger brothers, though in any case he had to house the mother of the man who had been there before him. Then came a failure in the business of the little town—the making of velvet—and though there were other rich communities that would have liked to claim him, he was true to his own impoverished flock, and set forth like a pilgrim in search of aid for them. In this apostolic journey he visited Holland and England as well as Germany, and it was in London that, in Elizabeth Fry, he found a noble kindred spirit, much older, of course, than himself, as we count the time of earth, but still full of all the tender enthusiasm of love's immortal youth.   Her wonderful work among the prisoners of New-gate sent him back to his own parish all on fire to help the prisoners of his own country, and he began at once with Düsseldorf, the prison nearest home.   Through him was founded the first German organization for improving the discipline of prisons.

Most of all he wanted to help the women who on leaving the prison doors were left without roof or protector.

With his own hands he made clean his old summer-house, and in this shelter—twelve feet square—which he had furnished with a bed, a chair, and a table, he asked the All-father to lead some poor outcast to the little home he had made for her.

It was at night that for the first time a poor forlorn creature came in answer to that prayer,

and he and his wife led her in to the place prepared for her. Nine others followed, and, by
the time the number had risen to twenty, a new
building was ready for them with its own field
and garden, and Fliedner's wife, helped by
Mademoiselle Gobel, who gave her services "all
for love and nothing for reward," had charge
of the home, where many a one who, like the
woman in the Gospel, "had been a great sinner"
began to lead a new life and to follow Christ.

For the children of some of these women a
kindergarten arose; but the work of all others
on which the pastor's heart was set was the
training of women to nurse and tend the poor;
for in his own parish, where there was much
illness and ignorance, there was no one to do
this. Three years after his earlier venture, in
1836 when Miss Nightingale in her far-away
home was a girl of sixteen still more or less
in the schoolroom, this new undertaking was
begun, this quiet haven, from which her own
great venture long afterwards took help and
teaching, was built up by this German saint.

The failure of the velvet industry at Kaiserswerth, in the pastor's first year, had left an empty factory which he turned into a hospital.

But when it was opened, the faith needed was much like the faith of Abraham when great blessing was promised to a son whom the world thought he would never possess; for the Deaconess Hospital, when the wards were fitted up by its pastor with "mended furniture and cracked earthenware," had as yet no patients and no deaconesses.

There is, however, one essential of a good hospital which can be bought by labour as well as by money; and by hard work the hospital was kept admirably clean.

The first patient who knocked at its doors was a servant girl, and other patients followed so quickly that within the first year sixty patients were nursed there and seven nurses had entered as deaconess and probationers. All the deaconesses were to be over twenty-five, and though they entered for five years, they could leave at any moment. The code of rules drawn up by the pastor was very simple, and there were not any vows; but the form of admission was a solemn one and included the laying on of hands, while the pastor invoked the Threefold Name, saying : " May God the Father, the Son, and the Holy Ghost, three Persons in one God, bless you ; may He stablish you in the Truth until death, and give you hereafter the Crown of Life.   Amen."

It all had a kind of homely grace, even in outward things. The deaconesses wore a large white turned-down collar over a blue cotton gown, a white muslin cap tied on under the chin with a large bow, and a white apron—a dress so well suited to the work that young and old both looked more than usually sweet and womanly in it.

The story of how the deaconesses found a head, and Fliedner a second helper after the death of his first wife, reads rather like a Hans Andersen fairy tale.

He travelled to Hamburg to ask Amalie Sievekin to take charge of the Home, and as she could not do so, she advised him to go to her friend and pupil Caroline Berthean, who had had experience of nursing in the Hamburg Hospital.

The pastor was so pleased with Miss Caroline that he then and there offered her the choice of becoming either his wife or the Superintendent of the Deaconesses' Home.

She said she would fill *both* the vacant places, and their honeymoon was spent in Berlin that they might "settle" the first five deaconesses in the Charité Hospital.

Caroline, young though she was, made a good Deaconess Mother,* and she seems also to have been an excellent wife, full of devotion to the work her husband loved, through all the rest of her life. The deaconesses give their work, and in a sense give themselves. They do not pay for their board, but neither are they paid for their work, though they are allowed a very simple yearly outfit of two cotton gowns and aprons, and every five years a new *best* dress of blue woollen material and an apron of black alpaca. Also their outdoor garb of a long black cloak and bonnet is supplied to them, and each is

---

* For a charming sketch of Fliedner's first wife, a woman of rare excellence, my readers are referred to "A History of Nursing," by M. Adelaide Nutting, R.N., and Lavinia P. Dock, R.N. (G. P. Putnam and Sons.)

allowed a little pocket money. Their private property remains their own to control as they please, whether they live or die.

The little account of Kaiserswerth which Miss Nightingale wrote is most rare and precious, having long been out of print, but from the copy in the British Museum I transfer a few sentences to these pages, because of their quaintness and their interest for all who are feeling their way in the education of young children :—

" In the Orphan Asylum," wrote Miss Nightingale, " each family lives with its deaconess exactly as her children. Some of them have already become deaconesses or teachers, some have returned home. When a new child is admitted, a little feast celebrates its arrival, at which the pastor himself presides, who understands children so well that his presence, instead of being a constraint, serves to make the little new-comer feel herself at home. She chooses what is to be sung, she has a little present from the pastor, and, after tea, at the end of the evening, she is prayed for. . . .

"One morning, in the boys' ward, as they were about to have prayers, just before breakfast, two of the boys quarrelled about a hymn book. The 'sister' was uncertain, for a moment, what to do. They could not pray in that state of mind, yet excluding them from the prayer was not likely to improve them. She told a story of her own childhood, how one night she had been cross with her parents, and, putting off her prayers till she felt good again, had fallen asleep. The children were quite silent for a moment and shocked at the idea that anybody should go to bed without praying. The two boys were reconciled, and prayers took place. . . ."

In the British Museum also is a copy of the following letter :—

"MESSRS. DUBAW,—A gentleman called here yesterday from you, asking for a copy of my 'Kaiserswerth' for, I believe, the British Museum.

"Since yesterday a search has been instituted—but only two copies have been found, and one of those is torn and dirty. I send you the least bad-looking. You will see the date is 1851, and after the copies then printed were given away I don't think I have ever thought of it.

"I was twice in training there myself. Of course, since then hospital and district nursing have made great strides. Indeed, district nursing has been invented.

"But never have I met with a higher love, a purer devotion than there. There was no neglect.

"It was the more remarkable because many of the deaconesses had been only peasants (none were gentlewomen when I was there).

"The food was poor—no coffee but bean coffee—no luxury but cleanliness.

"FLORENCE NIGHTINGALE."

CHAPTER VII.

Years of preparation.

FLORENCE NIGHTINGALE, like Felicia Skene, had that saving gift of humour which at times may make bearable an otherwise unbearable keenness of vision.

Here, for instance, is her account of the customary dusting of a room in those days (is it always nowadays so entirely different as might be wished?) :—

" Having witnessed the morning process called 'tidying the room' for many years, and with ever-increasing astonishment, I can describe what it is. From the chairs, tables, or sofa, upon which 'things' have lain during the night, and which are therefore comparatively clean from dust or blacks, the poor 'things' having 'caught it,' they are removed to other chairs, tables, sofas, upon which you could write your name with your finger in the dust or blacks. The other side of the things is therefore now evenly dirtied or dusted. The housemaid then flaps everything or some things not out of her reach with a thing called a duster—the dust flies up, then resettles more equally than it lay before the operation. The room has now been 'put to rights.'"

You see the shrewd humour of that observation touches the smallest detail. Miss Nightingale never wasted time in unpractical theorizing. In discussing the far-off attainment of ideal nursing she says :—

"Will the top of Mont Blanc ever be made habitable? Our answer would be, it will be many thousands of years before we have reached the bottom of Mont Blanc in making the earth healthy. Wait till we have reached the bottom before we discuss the top."

Did she with her large outlook and big heart see our absurdity as well as our shame when,

pointing a finger of scorn at what we named the
superstition of other countries, we were yet content to see Spain and France and Italy sending
out daily, in religious service to the poor, whole
regiments of gentle and refined women trained
in the arts of healing and the methods of discipline, while even in our public institutions—
our hospitals and workhouses and prisons—it
would hardly have been an exaggeration to say
that most of the so-called "nurses" of those
days were but drunken sluts?

She herself has said :—

"Shall the Roman Catholic Church do all the
work? Has not the Protestant the same Lord,
who accepted the services not only of men, but
also of women?"

One saving clause there is for England concerning this matter in the history of that time,
in the work of a distinguished member of the
Society of Friends, even before Florence Nightingale or Felicia Skene had been much heard
of. We read that "the heavenly personality of
Elizabeth Fry (whom Miss Nightingale sought

out and visited) was an ever-present inspiration
in her life." From Elizabeth Fry our heroine
heard of Pastor Fliedner's training institute for
nurses at Kaiserswerth, already described in the
foregoing chapter; but, before going there, she
took in the meantime a self-imposed course of
training in Britain, visiting the hospitals in
London, Edinburgh, and Dublin, though, so far
as the nursing was concerned, the criticisms in
her own *Nursing Notes* of later years would
certainly suggest that what she learned was
chiefly what *not* to do. Her gracious and win
ning dignity was far indeed from the blindness
of a weak amiability, and it can hardly be
doubted that what she saw of the so-called
" nurses" in our hospitals of those days, went
far to deepen her resolve to devote herself to
a calling then in dire neglect and disrepute.
Dirt, disorder, drunkenness—these are the words
used by a trustworthy biographer in describing
the ways of English nurses in those days—of
whom, indeed, we are told that they were of
a very coarse order—ill-trained, hard-hearted,
immoral. There must surely have been excep-

tions, but they seem to have been so rare as to have escaped notice. Indeed, it was even said that in those days—so strong and stupefying is the force of custom—decent girls avoided this noble calling, fearing to lose their character if found in its ranks.

But whatever were Florence Nightingale's faults—and she was by no means so inhuman as to be without faults — conventionality of thought and action certainly cannot be counted among them; and what she saw of the poor degraded souls who waited on the sick in our hospitals did but strengthen her resolve to become a nurse herself.

Since she found no good school of nursing in England, she went abroad, and visited, among other places, the peaceful old hospital of St. John at Bruges, where the nuns are cultivated and devoted women who are well skilled in the gentle art of nursing.

To city after city she went, taking with her not only her gift of discernment, but also that open mind and earnest heart which made of her life-offering so world-wide a boon.

I do not think I have used too strong a word of the gift she was preparing. For the writer of an article which appeared in *Nursing Notes** was right when, at the end of Miss Nightingale's life, she wrote of her :—

" Miss Nightingale belongs to that band of the great ones of the earth who may be acclaimed as citizens of the world ; her influence has extended far beyond the limits of the nation to which she owed her birth, and in a very special sense she will be the great prototype for all time to those who follow more especially in her footsteps, in the profession she practically created. We must ever be grateful for the shining example she has given to nurses, who in her find united that broad-minded comprehension of the ultimate aim of all their work, with a patient and untiring devotion to its practical detail, which alone combine to make the perfect nurse."

But as yet she was only humbly and diligently preparing herself for the vocation to which she

* The reference here is not to Miss Nightingale's book, but to the periodical which at present bears that name.

had determined, in face of countless obstacles, to devote herself, little knowing how vast would be the opportunities given to her when once she was ready for the work.

During the winter and spring of 1849–50 she made a long tour through Egypt with Mr. and Mrs. Bracebridge. On her way there she met in Paris two Sisters of the Order of St. Vincent de Paul, from whom she took introductions to the schools and " miséricorde " in Alexandria. There she saw the fruits of long and self-denying discipline among the Nursing Sisters, and in the following year she visited Pastor Fliedner's Institute at Kaiserswerth, where, among Protestant deaconesses, the life of ordered simplicity and service showed some of the same virtues.

Miss Nightingale's first visit to Kaiserswerth was comparatively short, but in the following year, 1852, she went there again and took four months of definite training, from June to October.

A deep and warm regard seems to have arisen between the Fliedners and their English pupil, and the pastor's friendship for Miss Nightingale's revered counsellor, Elizabeth Fry, must have been one pleasant link in the happy bond.

Fliedner was certainly a wonderful man, and Miss Nightingale's comment on the spirit of his work was as true as it was witty. " Pastor Fliedner," she said, " began his work with two beds under a roof, not with a castle in the air, and Kaiserswerth is now diffusing its blessings and its deaconesses over almost every Protestant land." This was literally true. Within ten years of founding Kaiserswerth he had established sixty nurses in twenty-five different centres. Later he founded a Mother-house on Mount Zion at Jerusalem, having already settled some of his nurses at Pittsburg in the United States. The building for the Jerusalem Mother-house was given by the King of Prussia, and, nursing all sick people, without any question of creed, is a school of training for nurses in the East.

Alexandria, Beyrout, Smyrna, Bucharest—he visited them all, and it is due to his efforts nearer home that to-day in almost all German towns of any importance there is a Deaconess

Home, sending out trained women to nurse in middle-class families at very moderate fees, and ready to nurse the poor without any charge at all.

When, in 1864, " he passed to his glorious rest "—the words are Miss Nightingale's—there were already one hundred such houses, and during part of Miss Nightingale's visit to Kaiserswerth, Pastor Fliedner was away a good deal on the missionary journeys which spread the Deaconess Homes through Germany, but they met quite often enough for each to appreciate the noble character of the other. In all his different kinds of work for helping the poor she was eagerly interested, and it may be that some of her wise criticisms of district visiting in later years may have been suggested by the courtesy and good manners that ruled the visiting of poor homes at Kaiserswerth in which she shared. It was there also that she made warm friendship with Henrietta Frickenhaus, in whose training college at Kaiserswerth 400 pupils had already passed muster. It should be added that Henrietta Frickenhaus was the first schoolmistress of Kaiserswerth.

Mr. Sidney Herbert visited Kaiserswerth while Miss Nightingale was there, and when, in the great moment that came afterwards, he asked her to go out to the Crimea, he knew well how detailed and definite her training had been.

Pastor Fliedner's eldest daughter told Mrs. Tooley how vividly she recalled her father's solemn farewell blessing when Miss Nightingale was leaving Kaiserswerth ; laying his hands on her bent head and, with eyes that seemed to look beyond the scene that lay before him, praying that she might be stablished in the Truth till death, and receive the Crown of Life.

And even mortal eyes may read a little of how those prayers for her future were fulfilled.

She left vivid memories. " No one has ever passed so brilliant an examination," said Fliedner, " or shown herself so thoroughly mistress of all she had to learn, as the young, wealthy, and graceful Englishwoman." Agnes Jones, who was trained there before her work in Liverpool left a memorable record of life spent in self-denying service, tells how the workers at

Kaiserswerth longed to see Miss Nightingale again, how her womanliness and lovableness were remembered, and how among the sick people were those who even in dying blessed her for having led them to the Redeemer ; for throughout her whole life her religion was the very life of her life, as deep as it was quiet, the underlying secret of that compassionate self-detachment and subdued fire, without which her wit and shrewdness would have lost their absolving glow and underlying tenderness. Hers was ever the gentleness of strength, not the easy bending of the weak. She was a pioneer among women, and did much to break down the cruel limitations which, in the name of affection and tradition, hemmed in the lives of English girls in those days. Perhaps she was among the first of that day in England to realize that the Christ, her Master, who sent Mary as His first messenger of the Resurrection, was in a fine sense of the word " unconventional," even though He came that every jot and tittle of religious law might be *spiritually* fulfilled.

It was after her return to England from

Germany that she published her little pamphlet on Kaiserswerth, from which quotations have already been given.

Her next visit was to the Convent of St. Vincent de Paul in Paris, where the nursing was a part of the long-established routine, and while there she was able to visit the hospitals in Paris, and learned much from the Sisters in their organized work among the houses of the poor. In the midst of all this she was herself taken ill, and was nursed by the Sisters. Her direct and personal experience of their tender skill no doubt left its mark upon her own fitness. On her return home to complete her recovery, her new capacity and knowledge made a good deal of delighted talk in the cottages, and Mrs. Tooley tells us how it was rumoured that " Miss Florence could set a broken leg better than a doctor," and made the old rheumatic folk feel young again with her remedies, to say nothing of her "eye lotions," which "was enough to ruin the spectacle folk." She was always ahead of her time in her belief in simple rules of health and diet and hatred of all that continual

Florence Nightingale in 1854.

(From a drawing by H. M. B. C.)

use of drugs which was then so much in fashion, and she no doubt saw many interesting experiments at Matlock Bank in helping Nature to do her own work.

As soon as her convalescence was over she visited London hospitals, and in the autumn of 1852 those of Edinburgh and Dublin, having spent a part of the interval in her home at Embley, where she had again the pleasure of being near her friends the Herberts, with whose neighbourly work among the poor she was in fullest sympathy.

Her first post was at the Harley Street Home for Sick Governesses. She had been interested in many kinds of efforts on behalf of those who suffer ; Lord Shaftesbury's Ragged School labours, for instance, had appealed to her, and to that and other like enterprises she had given the money earned by her little book on Kaiserswerth. But she always had in view the one clear and definite aim—to fit herself in every possible way for competent nursing. It was on August 12, 1853, that she became Superintendent of the Harley Street institution, which is now known as the Florence Nightingale Hospital. It was founded in 1850 by Lady Canning, as a Home for Invalid Gentlewomen, and when an appeal was made to Miss Nightingale for money and good counsel, she gave in addition *herself* and became for a time the Lady Superintendent.

The hospital was intended mainly for sick governesses, for whom the need of such a home of rest and care and surgical help had sometimes arisen, but it had been mismanaged and was in danger of becoming a failure. There Miss Nightingale, we read, was to be found " in the midst of various duties of a hospital—for the Home was largely a sanatorium — organizing the nurses, attending to the correspondence, prescriptions, and accounts ; in short, performing all the duties of a hard-working matron, as well as largely financing the institution."

" The task of dealing with sick and querulous women," says Mrs. Tooley, "embittered and rendered sensitive and exacting by the unfortunate circumstances of their lives, was not an easy one, but Miss Nightingale had a calm and cheerful spirit which could bear with the infirmities of the weak. And so she laboured on in the dull house in Harley Street, summer and winter, bringing order and comfort out of a wretched chaos, and proving a real friend and helper to the sick and sorrow-laden women.

"At length the strain proved too much for her delicate body, and she was compelled most reluctantly to resign her task."

She had worked very hard, and was seldom seen outside the walls of the house in Harley Street. Though she was not there very long, the effect of her presence was great and lasting, and the Home, which has now moved to Lisson Grove, has increased steadily in usefulness, though it has of necessity changed its lines a little, because the High Schools and the higher education of women have opened new careers and lessened the number of governesses, especially helpless governesses. It gives aid far and wide to the daughters and other kindred of hard-worked professional men, men who are serving the world with their brains, and nobly seeking to give work and service of as good a kind as lies within their power, rather than to snatch at its exact value in coin, even if that were possible—and in such toil as theirs, whether they be teachers, artists, parsons, or themselves doctors, it is *not* possible ; for such work cannot be weighed in money.

Queen Alexandra is President, and last year 301 patients were treated, besides the 16 who were already within its walls when the new year began.

CHAPTER VIII.

The beginning of the war—A sketch of Sidney Herbert.

IT was on April 11, 1854, that war was declared by Russia, and four days later the invasion of the Ottoman Empire began. England and France were the sworn allies of Turkey, and though the war had begun with a quarrel about "a key and a trinket," the key and the trinket were, after all, symbols, just as truly as the flags for which men lay down their lives.

England had entrusted the cause of peace to those faithful lovers of peace, Lord Aberdeen, Mr. Gladstone, Mr. Cobden, and Mr. Bright; but no single man in our "constitutional" Government is in reality a free agent, and the peace-loving members of the Cabinet had been skilfully handled by the potent Lord Palmerston, and did not perceive soon enough that the understanding with Turkey and with France, into which they had drifted, must endanger the peace of Europe because the other Powers were ignored. If the English people had been secretly longing for war—and it is said that they had—then the terrible cup they had desired was to be drunk to the lees : the war on which they were entering was a war of agony and shame, a war in which men died by hundreds of neglect and mismanagement, before a woman's hand could reach the helm and reform the hospital ordinances in the ship of State.

Meanwhile, before we plunge into the horrors of the Crimean War we may rest our minds with a few pages about Miss Nightingale's friend, Mr. Sidney Herbert, who became an active and self-sacrificing power in the War Office.

When Florence Nightingale was born, Sidney Herbert—afterwards Lord Herbert of Lea—was already a boy of ten.

Those who know the outlook over the Thames, from the windows of Pembroke Lodge at Richmond, will realize that he too, like Florence Nightingale, was born in a very beautiful spot.

His father, the eleventh Earl of Pembroke, had married the daughter of Count Woronzow, the Russian Ambassador, and, in Sidney's knowledgeable help afterwards at the War Office during the Crimean War, it is not without interest to remember this.

His birth had not been expected so soon, and there were no baby clothes handy at Pembroke Lodge, where his mother was staying. It would seem that shops were not so well able to supply every need with a ready-made garment as they are in these days ; so the first clothes that the baby boy wore were lent by the workhouse until his own were ready.

In later days, when he cared for the needs of all who crossed his path, until his people feared —or pretended to fear—that he would give away all he had, his mother used to say that workhouse clothes were the first he had worn after his birth, and were also clearly those in which he would die.

He had good reason to rejoice in his lineage, for he was descended from the sister of Sir Philip Sidney, after whom he was named. He

too, like his great namesake, was all his life full
of that high courtesy which comes of loving
consideration for others rather than for self, and
is never more charming than in those who,
being in every sense "well-born," have seen it
in their fathers, and in their fathers before them,
notwithstanding that in those others who, less
fortunate, whether they be rich or poor, having
come of an ill brood, are yet themselves well-
bred, such courtesy is of the courts of heaven.

The boy's father had much individuality.
Being the owner of some thirty villages, and lord-
lieutenant of the county, he was naturally a
great magnate in Wiltshire. He was very fond
of dogs, and his favourites among them sat at
his own table, each with its own chair and plate.

Sidney was almost like an only son at home,
for his elder brother, who was, of course, the
heir to Lord Herbert's patrimony, had married
unhappily and lived abroad.

The little boy seems to have been really rather
like the little angels in Italian pictures, a child
with golden curls and big brown eyes, with the
look of love and sunshine gleaming out of them

that he kept all his life, and there is a letter of his mother's, describing a children's fancy dress ball, at which she dressed him up as a little cupid, with wings and a wreath of roses, and was very proud of the result. He was either too little to mind, or if he hated it, as so many boys would, he bore with it to please his mother, who, we are told, made as much of an idol of him as did the rest of his family. And indeed it is most wonderful, from all accounts, that he was not completely spoiled. Here is his mother's letter about it :—

"I never did see anything half so like an angel. I must say so, although it was my own performance. He had on a garland of roses and green leaves mixed ; a pair of wild duck's wings, put on wire to make them set well ; a bow and arrow, and a quiver with arrows in it, tied on with a broad blue ribbon that went across his sweet neck."

In another of her letters we are told of a visit paid, about this time, to Queen Charlotte, and how the child "Boysey" climbed into the Queen's lap, drew up and pulled down window-blinds, romped at hide-and-seek with the Duke of Cambridge, and showed himself to be not in the slightest degree abashed by the presence of royalty.

Lord Fitzwilliam, a friend and distant relation, used often to stay at Pembroke Lodge and at Wilton, and seems to have been pleased by the boy's courteous ways and winning looks ; for, having no children of his own, when he left most of his property to Lord Pembroke, the " remainder," which meant big estates in Ireland and Shropshire, was to go to his second son, Sidney.

The boy loved his father with a very special intimacy and tenderness, as we see by a letter written soon after he left Harrow and a little while before he went up to Oxford, where at Oriel he at once made friends with men of fine character and sterling worth. His father had died in 1827, and he writes from Chilmark, where the rector, Mr. Lear, was his tutor, and the Rectory was near his own old home at Wilton :—

" You cannot think how comfortable it is to be in a nice little country church after that great noisy chapel. Everything is so quiet and the people all so attentive that you might hear a pin fall while Mr. Lear is preaching. I like, too, being so near Wilton, so many things here ever bringing to mind all *he* said and did, all places where I have ridden with *him*, and the home where we used to be so happy. In short, there is not a spot about Wilton now which I do not love as if it were a person. I hope you will be coming there soon and get it over, for seeing that place again will be a dreadful trial to you."

Among his friends at Oxford were Cardinal Manning, Lord Lincoln, who as Duke of Newcastle was afterwards closely associated with him at the War Office ; Lord Elgin, Lord Dalhousie, and Lord Canning, all three Viceroys of India. It was there, too, that his friendship with Mr. Gladstone began. Lord Stanmore says that Mr. Gladstone told him a year or two before his death how one day at a University Convocation dealing with a petition against the Roman Catholic Relief Bill, to which he had himself gone as an under-graduate outsider, he had noticed among the crowd of undergraduates in the vestibule of the Convocation House "a tall and graceful figure, surmounted by a face of such singular sweetness and refinement that his attention was at once riveted by it, and with such force that the picture he then saw rose again as vividly before him while talking as when first seen sixty-eight years before." Mr. Gladstone inquired the name of this attractive freshman. "Herbert of Oriel," was the answer. They became friends; but in those days friendships between men of different colleges and different ages were not always easily kept up. The more intimate relations between himself and Herbert date only from a later time.

Herbert's noble and beautiful life was to be closely intertwined with that of his little friend and neighbour, in one of those friendships— holy in their unselfish ardour of comradeship and service of others—which put to shame many of the foolish sayings of the world, and prove that, while an ideal marriage is the divinest happiness God gives to earthly life, an ideal friendship also has the power to lift both joy and pain into the region of heaven itself.

This was a friendship which, as we shall see, arose in the first instance partly out of the fact that the two children grew up on neighbouring estates, and were both what Mrs. Tollemache has called " Sunday people "—people with leisure to give to others, as well as wealth ; and at the end of Sidney Herbert's life it was said that the following description of Sir Philip Sidney, after whom he was named, was in every particular a description of him :—

" He was gentle, loving, compassionate, forgiving as a woman, and yet had the dignity and valour of a man.   His liberality was so great that with him not to give was not to enjoy what he had.

" In his familiarity with men he never descended, but raised everybody to his own level. So modest, so humble was he, and so inaccessible to flattery, that he esteemed not praise except as an encouragement to further exertion in welldoing.   His tongue knew no deceit, and his mind no policy but frankness, courage, and sin-

cerity, and . . . England has had greater statesmen, but never so choice a union of the qualities
which make a Sidney.   His fame is founded on
those personal qualities of which his contem-
poraries were the best judges, although they may
not leave a trace in books or in history."

And of both might it most emphatically have
been said, as was said by Mr. Gladstone of one
of them: " Rare indeed—God only knows how
rare—are men with his qualities; but even a
man with his qualities might not have been so
happy as to possess his opportunities.   He had
them, and he used them."

The story of his betraying a State secret to that
other friend, who was the original of " Diana of
the Crossways," is a myth which has been more
than once disproved, and of which his biographer
says that any one who knew him, or knew the
real " Diana," would have treated it with derision.

But he was always ready to bear lightly
undeserved blame, just as he took it as of no
account when credit that should have been his
was rendered elsewhere.   Take, for instance, the

warrant which relieved soldiers of good conduct
from the liability of punishment by flogging.
He had worked hard at this warrant, and it
originated with him, although the Duke of
Cambridge supported him in it. But when one
of his friends expressed annoyance that the praise
had come to the better-known man, he replied
impatiently : " What *does* it matter who gets the
credit so long as the thing itself is done ? "

Nor did he ever seem to care about mere
material reward, and he simply could not understand the outcry of one useful servant of the
State who, when likely to be left out of office
in prospective Cabinet arrangements, exclaimed,
" And pray what is to become of *me* ? "

With him, as with Miss Nightingale, giving
was an untold and constant joy, and he was able
to be lavish because of his great personal economy
and self-denial. In all his beautiful home at
Wilton, Lord Stanmore tells us, his own were
the only rooms that could have been called bare
or shabby, and when he was urged to buy a good
hunter for himself, he had spent too much on
others to allow himself such a luxury. He

delighted in educating the sons of widows left
by men of his own order without means. "He
maintained," we read, "at one and the same time
boys at Harrow, Marlborough, and Woolwich,
another in training for an Australian career, and
a fifth who was being educated for missionary
work. And he expended much in sending poor
clergymen and their families to the seaside for a
month's holiday." And to gentlepeople who
were poor we read that the help of money "was
given so delicately as to remove the burden of
obligation. A thousand little attentions in time
of sickness or sorrow helped and cheered them.
In all these works his wife was his active co-
adjutor, but " we read that " it was not till after
his death that she was at all aware of their extent,
and even then not fully, so unostentatiously and
secretly were they performed. His sunny presence," says his biographer, "warmed and cheered
all around him, and the charm of his conversation
made him the light and centre of any company
of which he formed a part.* There are, however,

* "Memoir of Sidney Herbert," by Lord Stanmore. (John
Murray.)

many men who are brilliant and joyous in society, over whom a strange change comes when they cross their own threshold. Sidney Herbert was never more brilliant, never more charming, never more witty than when alone with his mother, his wife, his sisters, or his children.

" Nowhere was he seen to greater advantage than in his own home. He delighted in country life, and took a keen and almost boyish interest in its sports and pursuits, into the enjoyment of which he threw himself with a zest and fulness not common among busy men . . . a good shot, a bold rider, and an expert fisherman, he was welcomed by the country gentlemen as one of themselves, and to this he owed much of his great popularity in his own country. But it was also due to the unfailing consideration shown by him to those of every class around him, and the sure trust in his responsive sympathy which was felt by all, high and low alike, dwelling within many miles of Wilton. By all dependent on him, or in any way under his orders, he was adored, and well deserved to be so. The older servants were virtually members of his family, and he took much pains in seeing to their interests, and helping their children to start well in the world."

"Never," says Lady Herbert, "did he come down to Wilton, if only for a few days, without going to see Sally Parham, an old housemaid, who had been sixty years in the family, and Larkum, an old carpenter of whom he was very fond, and who on his death-bed gave him the most beautiful and emphatic blessing I ever heard."

Of his splendid work in the War Office, and for our soldiers long after he had laid aside War Office cares, we shall read in its due place. Meanwhile we think of him for the present as Florence Nightingale's friend, and her neighbour when in the south, for his beautiful Wilton home was quite near to her own home at Embley.

Before the Crimean War began he was already giving his mind to army reform, and while that war was in progress the horrors of insanitary carelessness, as he saw them through Florence Nightingale's letters, made of him England's greatest sanitary reformer in army matters, with the single exception of Florence Nightingale herself.

The two had from the first many tastes in common, and among those of minor importance was their great affection for animals.   He was as devoted to his horse Andover as she had been to the little owl Athene, of which her sister, Lady Verney, in an old MS. quoted by Sir Stuart Grant Duff, gives the following pretty history :—

" Bought for 6 lepta from some children into whose hands it had dropped out of its nest in the Parthenon, it was brought by Miss Nightingale to Trieste, with a slip of a plane from the Ilissus and a cicala.   At Vienna the owl ate the cicala and was mesmerized, much to the improvement of his temper.   At Prague a waiter was heard to say that ' this is the bird which all English ladies carry with them, because it tells them when they are to die.'   It came to England by Berlin, lived at Embley, Lea Hurst, and in London, travelled in Germany, and stayed at Carlsbad while its mistress was at Kaiserswerth. It died the very day she was to have started for Scutari (her departure was delayed two days), and the only tear that she had shed during that tremendous week was when —— put the little body into her hand. 'Poor little beastie,' she said, 'it was odd how much I loved you.'"

And we read that before his death, Lord Herbert with a like tenderness bade a special farewell to his horse Andover, kissing him on the neck, feeding him with sugar, and telling him he should never ride again.

That was when he was already extremely ill, though not too ill to take care that a young priest who was dying also, but too poor to buy all the doctor had ordered, should be cared for out of his own purse.

With him, as with Florence Nightingale, giving and helping seem to have been unceasing.

The friendship between them was very dear to both of them, and was warmly shared by Lord Herbert's wife. When they all knew that death was waiting with a summons, and that Lord Herbert's last journey abroad could have but one ending, even though, as things turned out, he was to have just a momentary

glimpse of home again, Florence Nightingale
was the last friend to whom he bade farewell.
But that was not till 1861, and in the inter-
vening years they worked incessantly together,
for the good of the army and the improvement
of sanitary conditions.

CHAPTER IX.

The Crimean muddle—Explanations and excuses.

In our last chapter we ended with a word about those sanitary reforms which were yet to come. How appalling was the ignorance and confusion in 1854, when the war in the Crimea began, has now become matter of common knowledge everywhere.

I note later, as a result of my talk with General Evatt, some of the reasons and excuses for the dire neglect and muddle that reigned. John Bull was, as usual, so arrogantly sure of himself that he had—also as usual—taken no sort of care to keep himself fit in time of peace, and there was no central organizing authority for the equipment of the army—every one was responsible, and therefore no one. The provisions bought by contract were many of them rotten and mouldy, so cleverly had the purchasers been deceived and defrauded. The clothing provided for the men before Sebastopol, where, in at least one instance, man was literally frozen to man, were such as would have been better suited to India or South Africa. Many of the boots sent out were fitter for women and children playing on green lawns than for the men who must tramp over rough and icy roads. The very horses were left to starve for want of proper hay. Proper medical provision there was none. There were doctors, some of them nobly unselfish, but few of them trained for that particular work. An army surgeon gets little practice in time of peace, and one lady, a Red Cross nurse, told me that even in our South African campaign the doctor with whom she did her first bit of bandaging out there told her he had not bandaged an arm for fifteen years! But indeed many of the doctors in the Crimea were not only badly prepared, they were also so tied up with red-tape details that, though they gave their lives freely, they quickly fell in with the helpless chaos of a hospital without a head.

England shuddered to the heart when at last

she woke up under the lash of the following letter from William Howard Russell, the *Times* war correspondent :—

"The commonest accessories of a hospital are wanting, there is not the least attention paid to decency or cleanliness, the stench is appalling . . . and, for all I can observe, the men die without the least effort to save them. There they lie just as they were let gently down on the ground by the poor fellows, the comrades, who brought them on their backs from the camp with the greatest tenderness, but who are not allowed to remain with them."

"Are there," he wrote at a later date, "no devoted women among us, able and willing to go forth and minister to the sick and suffering soldiers of the East in the hospitals at Scutari ? Are none of the daughters of England, at this extreme hour of need, ready for such a work of mercy ? . . . France has sent forth her Sisters of Mercy unsparingly, and they are even now by the bedsides of the wounded and the dying, giving what woman's hand alone can give of

comfort and relief. . . . Must we fall so far
below the French in self-sacrifice and devotedness,
in a work which Christ so signally blesses as done
unto Himself? 'I was sick and ye visited me.'"

What the art of nursing had fallen to in
England may be guessed from the fact lately
mentioned to me by a great friend of Miss
Nightingale's, that when Florence Nightingale
told her family she would like to devote her life
to nursing, they said with a smile, "Are you
sure you would not like to be a kitchen-maid?"

Yet the Nightingales were, on other questions,
such as that of the education of girls, far in
advance of their time.

Possibly nothing short of those letters to
the *Times*, touching, as they did, the very quick
of the national pride, could have broken down
the "Chinese wall" of that particular prejudice.

Something may be said at this point as to what
had been at the root of the dreadful condition of
things in the hospitals before Miss Nightingale's
arrival. I have had some instructive talk with
Surgeon-General Evatt, who knows the medical

administration of our army through and through, and whose friendship with Miss Nightingale arose in a very interesting way, but will be mentioned later on in its due place.

General Evatt has pointed out to me in conversation that what is still a weakness of our great London hospitals, though lessened there by the fierce light of public opinion that is ever beating upon them, was the very source of the evil at Scutari.

Such hospitals as the London, doing such magnificent work that it deserves a thousand times the support it receives, are, explained General Evatt, without any central authority. The doctors pay their daily visits and their code is a high one, but they are as varied in ability and in character as any other group of doctors, and are responsible to no one but God and their own conscience. The nursing staff have *their* duties and *their* code, but are under separate management. The committee secures the funds and manages the finance, but it is again quite distinct in its powers, and does not control either doctors or nurses.

The Barrack Hospital at Scutari was, said the General, in this respect just like a London hospital of sixty years ago, set down in the midst of the Crimea. There was, he said—to adapt a well-known quotation—"knowledge without authority, and authority without knowledge," but no power to unite them in responsible effort. Therefore we must feel deep pity, not indignation, with regard to any one member of the staff ; for each alone was helpless against the chaos, until Miss Nightingale, who stood outside the official muddle, yet with the friendship of a great War Minister behind her, and in her hand all the powers of wealth, hereditary influence, and personal charm, quietly cut some of the knots of red tape which were, as she saw clearly, strangling the very lives of our wounded soldiers. When I spoke of the miracle by which a woman who had been all her life fitting herself for this work, had suddenly received her world-wide opportunity, he replied : "Yes, I have often said it was as if a very perfect machine had through long years been fitted together and polished to the highest efficiency, and when, at last, it was ready for service, a hand was put forth to accept and use it."

Just as he sought to explain the awful condition of the army hospitals at the beginning of the war ; so also he, as a military doctor, pointed out to me that there were even many excuses for the condition of the transport service, and the idiotic blunders of a government that sent soldiers to the freezing winters of the Crimea in clothes that would have been better suited to the hot climate of India.

The army after the Peninsular War had been split up into battalions, and had, like the hospitals, lost all *centre* of authority. England had been seething with the social troubles of our transition from the feudal order to the new competitions and miseries of a commercial and mechanical age. Machinery was causing uproar among the hand-workers. Chartist riots, bread riots, were upsetting the customary peace. Troops were sent hither and thither, scattered over the country, and allowed a certain degree of licence and slackness. The army had no administrative head. There was no one to consider the

question of stores or transit, and, even when the
war broke out, it was treated with John Bull's
too casual self-satisfaction as a moment of
excitement and self-glorification, from which
our troops were to return as victors in October,
after displaying themselves for a few weeks and
satisfactorily alarming the enemy.   The moral of
it all is ever present and needs no pressing home.
Not until every man has had the training of a
man in defence of his own home, and is himself
responsible for the defence of his own hearth,
shall we as a nation learn the humility and
caution of the true courage, and realize how
much, at the best, is outside human control, and
how great is our responsibility in every detail for
all that lies within it.

CHAPTER X.

" Five were wise, and five foolish."

WHEN the great moment came, there was one wise virgin whose lamp had long been trimmed and daily refilled with ever finer quality of flame. She was not alone. There were others, and she was always among the first to do them honour. But she stood easily first, and first, too, in the modesty of all true greatness. All her life had been a training for the work which was now given to her hand.

Among the many women who longed to nurse and tend our soldiers, many were fast bound by duties to those dependent on them, many were tied hand and foot by the pettifogging prejudices of the school in which they had been brought up. Many, whose ardour would have burned up all prejudice and all secondary claim, were yet ignorant, weak, incapable. Florence Nightingale, on the contrary, was highly trained, not only in intellect, but in the details of what she rightly regarded as an art, "a craft," the careful art of nursing—highly disciplined in body and in soul, every muscle and nerve obedient to her will, an international linguist, a woman in whom organizing power had been developed to its utmost capacity by a severely masculine education, and whose experience had been deepened by practical service both at home and abroad.

Her decision was a foregone conclusion, and a very striking seal was set upon it. For the letter, in which she offered to go out to the Crimea as the servant of her country, was crossed by a letter from Mr. Sidney Herbert, that country's representative at the War Office, asking her to go. Promptitude on both sides had its own reward ; for each would have missed the honour of spontaneous initiative had there been a day's delay.

Here is a part of Mr. Herbert's letter :—

"*October* 15, 1854.

" DEAR MISS NIGHTINGALE,—You will have

seen in the papers that there is a great deficiency
of nurses at the hospital of Scutari. The other
alleged deficiencies, namely, of medical men, lint,
sheets, etc., must, if they ever existed, have been
remedied ere this, as the number of medical officers
with the army amounted to one to every ninety-
five men in the whole force, being nearly double
what we have ever had before ; and thirty more
surgeons went out there three weeks ago, and
must at this time, therefore, be at Constantinople.
A further supply went on Monday, and a fresh
batch sail next week. As to medical stores, they
have been sent out in profusion, by the ton
weight—15,000 pair of sheets, medicine, wine,
arrowroot in the same proportion ; and the only
way of accounting for the deficiency at Scutari,
if it exists, is that the mass of the stores went to
Varna, and had not been sent back when the
army left for the Crimea, but four days would
have remedied that.

"In the meantime, stores are arriving, but the
deficiency of female nurses is undoubted ; none
but male nurses have ever been admitted to
military hospitals. It would be impossible to

carry about a large staff of female nurses with an army in the field. But at Scutari, having now a fixed hospital, no military reason exists against the introduction ; and I am confident they might be introduced with great benefit, for hospital orderlies must be very rough hands, and most of them, on such an occasion as this, very inexperienced ones.

" I receive numbers of offers from ladies to go out, but they are ladies who have no conception of what a hospital is, nor of the nature of its duties; and they would, when the time came, either recoil from the work or be entirely useless, and consequently, what is worse, entirely in the way ; nor would these ladies probably even understand the necessity, especially in a military hospital, of strict obedience to rule, etc. . . .

" There is but one person in England that I know of who would be capable of organizing and superintending such a scheme, and I have been several times on the point of asking you hypothetically if, supposing the attempt were made, you would undertake to direct it. The selection of the rank and file of nurses would be difficult—no one knows that better than yourself. The difficulty of finding women equal to the task, after all, full of horror, and requiring, besides knowledge and goodwill, great knowledge and great courage, will be great; the task of ruling them and introducing system among them great; and not the least will be the difficulty of making the whole work smoothly with the medical and military authorities out there.

"This is what makes it so important that the experiment should be carried out by one with administrative capacity and experience. A number of sentimental, enthusiastic ladies turned loose in the hospital at Scutari would probably after a few days be *mises à la porte* by those whose business they would interrupt, and whose authority they would dispute.

"My question simply is—would you listen to the request to go out and supervise the whole thing? You would, of course, have plenary authority over all the nurses, and I think I could secure you the fullest assistance and co-operation from the medical staff, and you would also have an unlimited power of drawing on the Government for whatever you think requisite for the success of your mission. On this part of the subject the details are too many for a letter, and I reserve it for our meeting; for, whatever decision you take, I know you will give me every assistance and advice. I do not say one word to press you. You are the only person who can judge for yourself which of conflicting or incompatible duties is the first or the highest; but I think I must not conceal from you that upon your decision will depend the ultimate success or failure of the plan. . . . Will you let me have a line at the War Office, to let me know?

"There is one point which I have hardly a right to touch upon, but I trust you will pardon me. If you were inclined to undertake the great work, would Mr. and Mrs. Nightingale consent? This work would be so national, and the request made to you, proceeding from the Government which represents the nation, comes at such a moment that I do not despair of their consent.

"Deriving your authority from the Government, your position would ensure the respect and consideration of every one, especially in a service where official rank carries so much respect. This would secure you any attention or comfort on your way out there, together with a complete submission to your orders. I know these things are a matter of indifference to you, except so far as they may further the great object you may have in view; but they are of importance in themselves, and of every importance to those who have a right to take an interest in your personal position and comfort.

"I know you will come to a right and wise decision. God grant it may be one in accordance with my hopes.—Believe me, dear Miss Nightingale, ever yours,   SIDNEY HERBERT."

Miss Nightingale's decision was announced in the *Times*, and on October 23 the following paragraph appeared in that paper:—

"It is known that Miss Nightingale has been appointed by Government to the office of Superintendent of Nurses at Scutari. She has been pressed to accept of sums of money for the general objects of the hospitals for the sick and wounded. Miss Nightingale neither invites nor can refuse these generous offers. Her bankers' account is opened at Messrs. Glyn's, but it must be understood that any funds forwarded to her can only be used so as not to interfere with the official duties of the Superintendent."

This was written by Miss Nightingale herself, and the response in money was at once very large, but money was by no means the first or most difficult question.

No time must be lost in choosing the nurses who were to accompany the Lady-in-Chief. It was not until later that she became known by that name, but it already well described her office, for every vital arrangement and decision seems to have centred in her. She knew well that her task could be undertaken in no spirit of lightness, and she never wasted power in mere fuss or flurry.

She once wrote to Sir Bartle Frere of "that careless and ignorant person called the Devil," and she did not want any of his careless and ignorant disciples to go out with her among her chosen band. Nor did she want any incompetent sentimentalists of the kind brought before us in that delightful story of our own South African War, of the soldier who gave thanks for the offer to wash his face, but confessed that fourteen other ladies had already offered the same service. Indeed, the rather garish merriment of that little tale seems almost out of place when we recall the rotting filth and unspeakable stench of blood and misery in which the men wounded in the Crimea were lying wrapped from head to foot. No antiseptic surgery, no decent sanitation, no means of ordinary cleanliness, were as yet found for our poor Tommies, and Kinglake assures us that all the efforts of masculine organization, seeking to serve the crowded hospitals with something called a laundry, had only succeeded in washing *seven* shirts for the entire army !

Miss Nightingale knew a little of the vastness of her undertaking, but she is described by Lady Canning at this critical time as " gentle and wise and quiet "—" in no bustle or hurry." Yet within a single week from the date of Mr. Herbert's

letter asking her to go out, all her arrangements
were made and her nurses chosen—nay more,
the expedition had actually started.

The War Office issued its official intimation
that "Miss Nightingale, a lady with greater
practical experience of hospital administration
and treatment than any other lady in this country,"
had undertaken the noble and arduous work of
organizing and taking out nurses for the soldiers;
and it was also notified that she had been
appointed by Government to the office of Superintendent of Nurses at Scutari.

The *Examiner* published a little biographical
sketch in reply to the question which was being
asked everywhere. Society, of course, knew Miss
Nightingale very well, but Society includes only
a small knot of people out of the crowd of
London's millions, to say nothing of the pro-
vinces. Many out of those millions were asking,
"Who is Miss Nightingale?" and, in looking
back, it is amazing to see how many disapproved
of the step she was taking.

In those days, as in these, and much more
tyrannically than in these, Mrs. Grundy had her

silly daughters, ready to talk slander and folly about any good woman who disregarded her. To Miss Nightingale she simply did not exist. Miss Martineau was right when she wrote of her that " to her it was a small thing to be judged by man's judgment."

And the spirit in which she chose the women who were to go out under her to the Crimea may be judged by later words of her own, called forth by a discussion of fees for nurses—words in which the italics are mine, though the sentence is quoted here to show the scorn she poured on fashion's canting view of class distinction.

" I have seen," she said, " somewhere in print that nursing is a profession to be followed by the ' lower middle-class.' Shall we say that painting or sculpture is a profession to be followed by the ' lower middle-class ' ? *Why limit the class at all?* Or shall we say that God is only to be served in His sick by the ' lower middle-class ' ?

" *It appears to be the most futile of all distinctions to classify as between ' paid ' and unpaid art, so between ' paid ' and unpaid nursing, to make into a*

*test a circumstance as adventitious as whether the hair
is black or brown—viz., whether people have private
means or not, whether they are obliged or not to work
at their art or their nursing for a livelihood.* Probably no person ever did that well which he did
only for money. Certainly no person ever did
that well which he did not work at as hard as
if he did it solely for money. If by amateur in
art or in nursing are meant those who take it
up for play, it is not art at all, it is not nursing
at all. *You never yet made an artist by paying him
well; but an artist ought to be well paid.*"

The woman who in later life wrote this, and
all her life acted on it, could not only well afford
to let *Punch* have his joke about the nightingales
who would shortly turn into ringdoves—although,
indeed, *Punch's* verses and illustration were delightful in their innocent fun—but could even without
flinching let vulgar slander insinuate its usual
common-minded nonsense. She herself has
written in *Nursing Notes* :—

"The everyday management of a large ward,
let alone of a hospital, the knowing what are the

laws of life and death for men, and what the laws
of health for wards (and wards are healthy or unhealthy mainly according to the knowledge or
ignorance of the nurse)—are not these matters
of sufficient importance and difficulty to require
learning by experience and careful inquiry, just
as much as any other art? They do not come
by inspiration to the lady disappointed in love,
nor to the poor workhouse drudge hard up for
a livelihood. And terrible is the injury which
has followed to the sick from such wild notions."

Happily, too, she was not blinded by the
narrow sectarian view of religion which was, in
her day and generation, so often a part of the
parrot belief of those who learned their English
version of the faith by rote, rather than with the
soul's experience, for she goes on to say :—

" In this respect (and why is it so?) in Roman
Catholic countries, both writers and workers are,
in theory at least, far before ours. They would
never think of such a beginning for a good-
working Superior or Sister of Charity. And
many a Superior has refused to admit a postulant

who appeared to have no better 'vocation' or reasons for offering herself than these.

"It is true we make no 'vows.' But is a 'vow' necessary to convince us that the true spirit for learning any art, most especially an art of charity, aright, is not a disgust to everything or something else? Do we really place the love of our kind (and of nursing as one branch of it) so low as this? What would the Mère Angélique of Port Royal, what would our own Mrs. Fry, have said to this?"

How silly, in the light of these words, was the gossip of the idle person, proud of her shopping and her visiting list and her elaborate choice of dinner, who greeted the news of this nursing embassy to the Crimea with such cheap remarks as that the women would be all invalided home in a month; that it was most improper for "young ladies"—for it was not only shop assistants who were called "young ladies" in early Victorian days—to nurse in a military hospital; it was only nonsense to try and "nurse soldiers when they did not even yet know what it was to nurse a baby!"

Such folly would only shake its hardened old noddle on reading, in the *Times* reprint of the article in the *Examiner*, that Miss Nightingale was " a young lady of singular endowments both natural and acquired. In a knowledge of the ancient languages and of the higher branches of mathematics, in general art, science, and literature, her attainments are extraordinary. There is scarcely a modern language which she does not understand, and she speaks French, German, and Italian as fluently as her native English. She has visited and studied all the various nations of Europe, and has ascended the Nile to its remotest cataract. Young (about the age of our Queen), graceful, feminine, rich, popular, she holds a singularly gentle and persuasive influence over all with whom she comes in contact. Her friends and acquaintances are of all classes and persuasions, but her happiest place is at home, in the centre of a very large band of accomplished relatives."

Girton and Newnham, Somerville and Lady Margaret did not then exist. If any one had dreamed of them, the dream had not yet been recorded.   Perhaps its first recognized expression, in Tennyson's " Princess " in 1847, mingling as it does with the story of a war and of the nursing of wounded men, may have imperceptibly smoothed away a few coarse prejudices from the path Florence Nightingale was to tread, but far more effectually was the way cleared by her own inspiring personality.   Mrs. Tooley quotes from an intimate letter the following words : " Miss Nightingale is one of those whom God forms for great ends.   You cannot hear her say a few sentences—no, not even look at her—without feeling that she is an extraordinary being.   Simple, intellectual, sweet, full of love and benevolence, she is a fascinating and perfect woman.   She is tall and pale.   Her face is exceedingly lovely, but better than all is the soul's glory that shines through every feature so exultingly.   Nothing can be sweeter than her smile.   It is like a sunny day in summer."

She who advised other women to make ready for the business of their lives as men make ready had been for long years preparing herself, and there was therefore none of the nervous waste and excitement of those who in a moment of impulse take a path which to their ignorance is like leaping in the dark.

But she knew well how much must depend on those she took with her, and it was clear that many who desired to go were quite unfitted for the work.

With her usual clearsightedness she knew where to turn for help. Felicia Skene was among those whom she consulted and whose advice she found of good service. It has already been noted in these pages that Miss Skene had, without knowing it, been preparing one of the threads to be interwoven in that living tapestry in which Miss Nightingale's labours were to endure in such glowing colours. Like Miss Nightingale she had real intimacy with those outside her own order, and by her practical human sympathy understood life, not only in one rank, but in all ranks. By night as well as by day her door was open to the outcast, and in several life-stories she had played a part which saved some poor girl from suicide. Full of humour and romance, and a welcome guest in every society, she will be remembered longest for her work in rescuing others both in body and in soul, and you will remember that, on the two occasions when the cholera visited Oxford, she nursed the sick and the dying by day and by night, and did much to direct and organize the helpful work of others.   Miss Wordsworth speaks of her " innate purity of heart and mind," and says of her, " one always felt of her that she had been brought up in the best of company, as indeed she had."   It was just such women that Miss Nightingale needed—women who, in constant touch with what was coarse and hard, could never become coarse or hard themselves ; women versed in practical service and trained by actual experience as well as by hard-won knowledge.

Moreover, it chanced that after Miss Skene's labour of love in the cholera visitation, her niece, " Miss Janie Skene, then a girl of fifteen, who was staying in Constantinople with her parents, had gone with her mother to visit the wounded soldiers at Scutari.   Shocked by their terrible sufferings and the lack of all that might have eased their pain, she wrote

strongly to her grandfather, who sent her letter
to the *Times*, where it did much to stir up public
opinion."

" It struck Felicia," says Miss Rickards, "that
having with great pains trained her corps of
nurses for the cholera, they might now be utilized
at Scutari, her great desire being to go out
herself at the head of them. Had these events
occurred at the present day, when ideas have
changed as to what ladies, still young, may and
may not do in the way of bold enterprise,
perhaps she might have obtained her parents'
permission to go. As it was the notion
was too new and startling to be taken into
consideration ; and she had to content herself
with doing all she could at home to send out
others.

" Her zeal was quickened by a letter she
received from Lord Stratford de Redcliffe, who
had been much struck by her energy and ability,
urging her to do all she could in England to send
to the rescue.

" At once she set out as a pioneer in the

undertaking, delighted to encourage her nurses to take their part in the heroic task.

"Meantime Miss Nightingale was hard at work enlisting recruits, thankful to secure Felicia's services as agent at Oxford. She sent her friends Mr. and Mrs. Bracebridge down there, that they might inspect the volunteers and select the women they thought would be suitable.

"The interviews took place in Mr. Skene's dining-room, along the walls of which the candidates were ranged.

"Kind-hearted as Mrs. Bracebridge was, her proceedings were somewhat in the 'Off with their heads!' style of the famous duchess in 'Alice in Wonderland.' If the sudden questions fired at each in succession were not answered in a way that she thought quite satisfactory, 'She won't do; send her out,' was the decided command.

"And Felicia had to administer balm to the wounded feelings of the rejected." *

* "Felicia Skene of Oxford," by E. C. Rickards.

CHAPTER XI.

The Expedition.

OF the thirty-eight nurses who went out with Miss Nightingale, twenty-four had been trained in sisterhoods, Roman and Anglican, and of the remaining fourteen, some had been chosen in the first instance by Lady Maria Forrester, others by Miss Skene and Mrs. Bracebridge, but it must be supposed that the final decision lay always with Miss Nightingale.

The correspondence that had poured in upon her and upon Mr. Herbert was overwhelming, and there was a personal interview with all who seemed in the least degree likely to be admitted to her staff; so that she worked very hard, with little pause for rest, to get through her ever-increasing task in time. Each member of the staff undertook to obey her absolutely.

Among the many who were rejected, though

most were unsuitable for quite other reasons,
there were some who objected to this rule.
Many who were full of sympathy and generosity
had to be turned away, because they had not had
enough training.   Advertisements had appeared
in the *Record* and the *Guardian*, but the crowd
of fair ladies who flocked to the War Office in
response were not always received with such
open arms as they expected.   Mr. Herbert was
well on his guard against the charms of im-
pulsive, but ignorant, goodwill, and he issued a
sort of little manifesto in which he said that
" many ladies whose generous enthusiasm prompts
them to offer services as nurses are little aware
of the hardships they would have to encounter,
and the horrors they would have to witness.
Were all accepted who offer," he added, with a
touch of humour, " I fear we should have not
only many indifferent nurses, but many hysterical
patients."

He and his wife were untiring in their efficiency and their help.

The English Sisterhoods had made a difficulty
about surrendering control over the Sisters they

sent out, but Miss Nightingale overcame that, and the Roman bishop entirely freed the ten Sisters of his communion from any rule which could clash with Miss Nightingale's orders.

It was on the evening of October 21, 1854, that the "Angel Band," as Kinglake rightly names them, quietly set out under cover of darkness, escorted by a parson and a courier and by Miss Nightingale's friends, Mr. and Mrs. Bracebridge of Atherstone Hall.

In this way all flourish of trumpets was avoided. Miss Nightingale always hated public fuss—or, indeed, fuss of any kind. She was anxious also to lighten the parting for those who loved her best, and who had given a somewhat doubting consent to her resolve.

The Quakerish plainness of her black dress did but make the more striking the beauty of her lovely countenance, the firm, calm sweetness of the smiling lips and steadfast eyes, the grace of the tall, slender figure; and as the train whirled her out of sight with her carefully-chosen regiment, she left with her friends a vision of good cheer and high courage.

But however quiet the setting forth, the arrival at Boulogne could not be kept a secret, and the enthusiasm of our French allies for those who were going to nurse the wounded made the little procession a heart-moving triumph. A merry band of white-capped fishwives met the boat and, seizing all the luggage, insisted on doing everything for nothing. Boxes on their backs and bags in their hands, they ran along in their bright petticoats, pouring out their hearts about their own boys at the front, and asking only the blessing of a handshake as the sole payment they would take. Then, as Miss Nightingale's train whistled its noisy way out of the station, waving their adieus while the tears streamed down the weather-beaten cheeks of more than one old wife, they stood and watched with longing hearts. At Paris there was a passing visit to the Mother-house of Miss Nightingale's old friends, the Sisters of St. Vincent de Paul, and a little call on Lady Canning, also an old friend, who writes of her as "happy and stout-hearted."

The poor "Angels" had a terrible voyage to

Malta, for the wind, as with St. Paul, was "contrary" and blew a hurricane dead against them, so that their ship, the *Vectis*, had something of a struggle to escape with its many lives. They touched at Malta on October 31, 1854, and soon afterwards set sail again for Constantinople.

What an old-world story it seems now to talk of "setting sail"!

On the 4th of November, the day before the battle of Inkermann, they had reached their goal, and had their work before them at Scutari.

A friend of mine who knows Scutari well has described it in summer as a place of roses, the very graves wreathed all over with the blossoming briars of them; and among those graves she found a nameless one, on which, without revealing identity, the epitaph stated, in the briefest possible way, that this was the grave of a hospital matron, adding in comment the words spoken of Mary when she broke the alabaster box—and in this instance full of pathos—the six words, "She hath done what she could." And I find from one of Miss Nightingale's letters that it was she herself who inscribed those words.

Unspeakable indeed must have been the difficulties with which any previous hospital matron had to contend, rigid and unbreakable for ordinary fingers the red tape by which she must have been bound. On this subject Kinglake has written words which are strong indeed in their haunting sincerity.

He writes of an " England officially typified that swathes her limbs round with red tape," and of those who, though dogged in routine duty, were so afraid of any new methods that they were found "surrendering, as it were, at discretion, to want and misery" for those in their care.

" But," he adds, " happily, after a while, and in gentle, almost humble, disguise which put foes of change off their guard, there acceded to the State a new power.

"Almost at one time—it was when they learnt how our troops had fought on the banks of the Alma—the hearts of many women in England, in Scotland, in Ireland, were stirred with a heavenly thought impelling them to offer and say that, if only the State were consenting, they would go out to tend our poor soldiers laid low on their hospital pallets by sickness or wounds; and the honour of welcoming into our public service this new and gracious aid belonged to Mr. Sidney Herbert."

He goes on to explain and define Mr. Herbert's exact position at the War Office; how he was not only official chief there, but, " having perhaps also learnt from life's happy experience that, along with what he might owe to fortune and birth, his capacity for business of State, his frank, pleasant speech, his bright, winning manners, and even his glad, sunshine looks, had a tendency to disarm opposition, he quietly, yet boldly, stepped out beyond his set bounds, and not only became in this hospital business the volunteer delegate of the Duke of Newcastle, but even ventured to act without always asking the overworked Department of War to go through the form of supporting him by orders from the Secretary of State; so that thus, and to the great advantage of the public service, he usurped, as it were, an authority which all who knew what he was doing rejoiced to see him wield. If he could not in strictness command by an official despatch, he at least could impart what he wished in a 'private letter;' and a letter, though ostensibly 'private,' which came from the War Office, under the hand of its chief, was scarce likely to encounter resistance from any official personages to whom the writer might send it.

"Most happily this gifted minister had formed a strong belief in the advantages our military hospitals would gain by accepting womanly aid; and, proceeding to act on this faith, he not only despatched to the East some chosen bands of ladies, and of salaried attendants accustomed to hospital duties, but also requested that they might have quarters and rations assigned to them; and, moreover, whilst requesting the principal medical officer at Scutari to point out to these new auxiliaries how best they could make themselves useful, Mr. Sidney Herbert enjoined him to receive with attention and deference the counsels of the Lady-in-Chief, who was, of course, no other than Miss Nightingale herself.

"That direction was one of great moment, and well calculated to govern the fate of a newly ventured experiment.

"Thus it was that, under the sanction of a government acceding to the counsels of one of its most alert and sagacious members, there went out angel women from England, resolved to confront that whole world of horror and misery that can be gathered into a military hospital from camp or battlefield; and their plea, when they asked to be trusted with this painful, this heart-rending mission, was simply the natural aptitude of their sex for ministering to those who lie prostrate from sickness and wounds. Using that tender word which likened the helplessness of the down-stricken soldier to the helplessness of infancy, they only said they would 'nurse' him; and accordingly, if regarded with literal strictness, their duty would simply be that of attendants in hospital wards—attendants obeying with strictness the orders of the medical officers.

"It was seen that the humble soldiers were likely to be the men most in want of care, and the ladies were instructed to abstain from attending upon any of the officers." *

* Kinglake's "Invasion of the Crimea," vol. vi. (William Blackwood and Sons.)

CHAPTER XII.

But before continuing the story of Miss Nightingale's expedition, we must turn aside for a moment in Kinglake's company to realize something of the devotion of another brave and unselfish Englishwoman who, without her " commanding genius," yet trod the same path of sacrifice and compassion. The words " commanding genius " were spoken by Dean Stanley of Miss Nightingale, and it is of Dean Stanley's sister Mary that a word must now be spoken. She had been the right hand of her father, the Bishop of Norwich, and, in serving the poor, had disclosed special gifts, made the more winning by her gentle, loving nature. Having had experience of travel, which was much less a thing of course than it is in these days, she was willing to escort a company of nurses chosen for work in the Levant, and at first this was all she expected to do. But there proved to be a difficulty about receiving them at Scutari, and she could not bring herself to leave them without guidance; so she quietly gave up all thought of returning to England while the war continued.

"Could she," asks Kinglake, "see them in that strait disband, when she knew but too well that their services were bitterly needed for the shiploads and shiploads of stricken soldiery brought down day by day from the seat of war? Under stress of the question thus put by her own exacting conscience, or perhaps by the simpler commandment of her generous heart, she formed the heroic resolve which was destined to govern her life throughout the long, dismal period of which she then knew not the end. Instead of returning to England, and leaving on the shores of the Bosphorus her band of sisters and nurses, she steadfastly remained at their head, and along with them entered at once upon what may be soberly called an appalling task—the task of 'nursing' in hospitals not only overcrowded with sufferers, but painfully, grievously wanting in most of the conditions essential to all good hospital management.

"The sisters and salaried nurses," says King-lake, "who placed themselves under this guidance were in all forty-six; and Miss Stanley, with great spirit and energy, brought the aid of her whole reinforcement—at first to the naval hospital newly founded at Therapia under the auspices of our Embassy, and afterwards to another establishment—to that fated hospital at Kullali, in which, as we saw, at one time a fearful mortality raged.

"Not regarding her mission as one that needs should aim loftily at the reformation of the hospital management, Miss Stanley submitted herself for guidance to the medical officers, saying, 'What do you wish us to do?' The officers wisely determined that they would not allow the gentle women to exhaust their power of doing good by undertaking those kinds of work that might be as well or better performed by men, and their answer was to this effect:

'The work that in surgical cases has been commonly done by our dressers will be performed by them, as before, under our orders. What we ask of you is that you will see the men take the medicines and the nourishment ordered for them, and we know we can trust that you will give them all that watchful care which alleviates suffering, and tends to restore health and strength.'

"With ceaseless devotion and energy the instructions were obeyed. What number of lives were saved—saved even in that pest-stricken hospital of Kullali—by a long, gentle watchfulness, when science almost despaired, no statistics, of course, can show; and still less can they gauge or record the alleviation of misery effected by care such as this; but apparent to all was the softened demeanour of the soldier when he saw approaching his pallet some tender, gracious lady intent to assuage his suffering, to give him the blessing of hope, to bring him the food he liked, and withal—when she came with the medicine— to rule him like a sick child.   Coarse expressions and oaths deriving from barracks and camps died

out in the wards as though exorcised by the
sacred spell of her presence, and gave way to
murmurs of gratitude.   When conversing in this
softened mood with the lady appointed to nurse
him, the soldier used often to speak as though
the worship he owed her and the worship he
owed to Heaven were blending into one senti-
ment ; and sometimes, indeed, he disclosed a wild
faith in the ministering angel that strained beyond the grave.   'Oh!' said one to the lady
he saw bending over his pallet, 'you are taking
me on the way to heaven; don't forsake me
now!'   When a man was under delirium, its
magic force almost always transported him to
the home of his childhood, and made him indeed
a child—a child crying, 'Mother! mother!'
Amongst the men generally, notwithstanding
their moments of fitful piety, there still glowed
a savage desire for the fall of Sebastopol.   More
than once—wafted up from Constantinople—
the sound of great guns was believed to announce
a victory, and sometimes there came into the
wards fresh tidings of combat brought down
from our army in front of the long-besieged

Florence Nightingale at the Therapia Hospital.

"I was sick, and ye visited me."

stronghold.   When this happened, almost all of
the sufferers who had not yet lost their conscious-
ness used to show that, however disabled, they
were still soldiers—true soldiers.   At such times,
on many a pallet, the dying man used to raise
himself by unwonted effort, and seem to yearn
after the strife, as though he would answer once
more the appeal of the bugles and drums."

Kinglake's touching description of what
womanly tenderness could do for our soldiers,
and of the worship it called forth, is followed
by these words :—

"But great would be the mistake of any
chronicler fancying that the advantage our
country derived from womanly aid was only an
accession of nurses; for, if gifted with the
power to comfort and soothe, woman also—a
still higher gift—can impel, can disturb, can
destroy pernicious content; and when she came
to the rescue in an hour of gloom and adversity,
she brought to her self-imposed task that fore-
thought, that agile brain power, that organizing
and governing faculty of which our country had

need. The males at that time in England were already giving proofs of the lameness in the use of brain power, which afterwards became more distinct. Owing, possibly, to their habits of industry, applied in fixed, stated directions, they had lost that command of brain force which kindles 'initiative,' and with it, of course, the faculty of opportunely resorting to any very new ways of action. They proved slow to see and to meet the fresh exigencies occasioned by war, when approaching, or even by war when present; and, apparently, in the hospital problem, they must have gone on failing and failing indefinitely, if they had not undergone the propulsion of the quicker—the woman's—brain to 'set them going' in time."

He then goes on to tell of the arrival at " the immense Barrack Hospital " at Scutari of Miss Nightingale and her chosen band. " If," he says, " the generous women thus sacrificing themselves were all alike in devotion to their sacred cause, there was one of them—the Lady-in-Chief —who not only came armed with the special ex-

perience needed, but also was clearly transcendent
in that subtle quality which gives to one human
being a power of command over others. Of
slender, delicate form, engaging, highly-bred,
and in council a rapt, careful listener, so long
as others were speaking; and strongly, though
gently, persuasive whenever speaking herself, the
Lady-in-Chief, the Lady Florence, Miss Nightingale, gave her heart to this enterprise in a
spirit of absolute devotion; but her sway was
not quite of the kind that many in England
imagined."

No, indeed! Sentimentalists who talk as
though she had been cast in the conventional
mould of mere yielding amiability, do not realize
what she had to do, nor with what fearless, un-
flinching force she went straight to her mark,
not heeding what was thought of herself, overlooking the necessary wounds she must give to
fools, caring only that the difficult duty should
be done, the wholesale agony be lessened, the
filth and disorder be swept away.

Her sweetness was the sweetness of strength,
not weakness, and was reserved not for the care-

less, the stupid, the self-satisfied, but for the men whose festering wounds and corrupting gangrene were suffered in their country's pay, and had been increased by the heedless muddle of a careless peace-time and a criminally mismanaged transport service.

The picture of their condition before her arrival is revolting in its horror. There is no finer thing in the history of this war, perhaps, than the heroism of the wounded and dying soldiers. We are told how, in the midst of their appalling privation, if they fancied a shadow on their General's face—as well, indeed, there might be, when he saw them without the common necessaries and decencies of life, let alone a sickroom—they would seize the first possible opening for assuring him they had all they needed, and if they were questioned by him, though they were dying of cold and hunger—

" No man ever used to say: ' My Lord, you see how I am lying wet and cold, with only this one blanket to serve me for bed and covering. The doctors are wonderfully kind, but they have not the medicines, nor the wine, nor any of the comforting things they would like to be given me. If only I had another blanket, I think perhaps I might live.' Such words would have been true to the letter."

But as for Lord Raglan, the chief whom they thus adored, " with the absolute hideous truth thus day by day spread out before him, he did not for a moment deceive himself by observing that no man complained."

Yet even cold and hunger were as nothing to the loathsome condition in which Miss Nightingale found the hospital at Scutari. There are certain kinds of filth which make life far more horrible than the brief moment of a brave death, and of filth of every sort that crowded hospital was full—filth in the air, for the stench was horrible, filth and gore as the very garment of the poor, patient, dying men.

There was no washing, no clean linen. Even for bandages the shirts had to be stripped from the dead and torn up to stanch the wounds of the living.

And there were other foul conditions which only the long labour of sanitary engineering could cure.

The arrival day by day of more and more of the wounded has been described as an avalanche. We all know Tennyson's " Charge of the Light Brigade " : that charge occurred at Balaclava the day before Miss Nightingale left England. And the terrible battle of Inkermann was fought the day after she arrived at Scutari.

Here is a word-for-word description from Nolan's history of the campaign, given also in Mrs. Tooley's admirable " Life " :—

" There were no vessels for water or utensils of any kind ; no soap, towels, or cloths, no hospital clothes ; the men lying in their uniforms, stiff with gore and covered with filth to a degree and of a kind no one could write about ; their persons covered with vermin, which crawled about the floors and walls of the dreadful den of dirt, pestilence, and death to which they were consigned.

" Medical assistance would naturally be expected by the invalid as soon as he found himself in a place of shelter, but many lay waiting for their turn until death anticipated the doctor. The medical men toiled with unwearied assiduity, but their numbers were inadequate to the work."

The great hospital at Scutari is a quadrangle, each wing nearly a quarter of a mile long, and built in tiers of corridors and galleries, one above the other. The wounded men had been brought in and laid on the floor, side by side, as closely as they could lie, so that Kinglake was writing quite literally when he spoke of "miles of the wounded."

Rotting beneath an Eastern sky and filling the air with poison, Miss Nightingale counted the carcasses of six dead dogs lying under the hospital windows. And in all the vast building there was no cooking apparatus, though it did boast of what was supposed to be a kitchen. As for our modern bathrooms, the mere notion would have given rise to bitter laughter; for even the homely jugs and basins were wanting in that palace of a building, and water of any kind was a rare treasure.

How were sick men to be "nursed," when they could not even be washed, and their very food had to be carried long distances and was usually the worst possible!

Miss Nightingale—the Lady-in-Chief—had the capacity, the will, the driving power, to change all that.

A week or two ago I had some talk with several of the old pensioners who remember her. The first to be introduced to me has lost now his power of speech through a paralytic stroke, but it was almost surprising, after all these long years that have passed between the Crimean day and our own day, to see how well-nigh overwhelming was the dumb emotion which moved the strong man at the naming of her name. The second, who was full of lively, chuckling talk, having been in active service for a month before her arrival in the Crimea, and himself seen the wondrous changes she wrought, was not only one of her adorers—all soldiers seem to be that —but also overflowing with admiration for her

capability, her pluck. To him she was not only
the ideal nurse, but also emphatically a woman
of unsurpassed courage and efficiency.

"You know, miss," he said, "there was a
many young doctors out there that should never
have been there—they didn't know their duty
and they didn't do as they should for us—and
she chased 'em, ay, she did that! She got rid
of 'em, and there was better ones come in their
place, and it was all quite different. Oh yes,"
and he laughed delightedly, as a schoolboy
might. "Oh yes, she hunted 'em out." I,
who have a great reverence for the medical
profession, felt rather shy and frightened and
inclined to blush, but the gusto with which the
veteran recalled a righteous vengeance on the
heads of the unworthy was really very funny.
And his gargoyle mirth set in high relief the
tenderness with which he told of Miss Nightingale's motherly ways with his poor wounded
comrades, and how she begged them not to
mind having their wounds washed, any more
than if she were really their mother or sister,
and thus overcame any false shame that might

have prevented their recovery. "Ah, she was a good woman," he kept repeating, "there's no two ways about it, a *good* woman!"

From Pensioner John Garrett of the 3rd Battalion Grenadier Guards, I had one very interesting bit of history at first hand; for he volunteered the fact that on his first arrival in the Crimea—which was evidently about the same time as Miss Nightingale's own, his first engagement having been the battle of Inkermann —Miss Nightingale being still unknown to the soldiers—a mere name to them—she had much unpopularity to overcome. Clearly jealous rumour had been at work against this mere woman who was coming, as the other pensioner had phrased it, "to chase the doctors." This, of course, made the completeness of her rapid victory over the hearts of the entire army the more noteworthy.

"And afterwards?" I asked.

"Oh, *afterwards we knew what she was*, and she was very popular indeed!" Though he treasured and carried about with him everywhere a Prayer Book containing Florence Nightingale's autograph—which I told him ought to be a precious heirloom to his sons and their children, and therefore refused to accept, when in the generosity of his kind old heart he thrice tried to press it upon me—he had only seen her once; for he was camping out at the front, and it was on one of her passing visits that he had his vision of her. He is a very young-looking old man of eighty-two, Suffolk-born, and had been in the army from boyhood up to the time of taking his pension. He had fought in the battle of Inkermann and done valiant trench-duty before Sebastopol, and confirmed quite of his own accord the terrible accounts that have come to us of the privations suffered. "Water," he said, "why, we could scarce get water to drink—much less to wash—why, I hadn't a change of linen all the winter through."

"And you hadn't much food, I hear, for your daily rations?" I said.

"Oh, we didn't have food every *day!*" said he, with a touch of gently scornful laughter. "Every *three* days or so, we may have had some biscuits served out. But there was a lot of the food as wasn't fit to eat."

He was, however, a man of few words, and when I asked him what Miss Nightingale was like, he answered rather unexpectedly and with great promptitude, " Well, she had a very nice figger." All the same, though he did not dilate on the beauty of her countenance, and exercised a certain reserve of speech when I tried to draw him out about the Lady-in-Chief, it was clear that hers was a sacred name to him, and that the bit of her handwriting which he possessed in the little book, so carefully unwrapped for me from the tin box holding his dearest possessions, which he uncorded under my eyes with his own capable but rather tired old hands, between two bouts of his wearying cough, had for long been the great joy and pride of his present quiet existence.

I had a talk with others of these veterans in their stately and well-earned home of rest in the Royal Hospital at Chelsea, and it was clear that to them all she was enshrined in memory's highest place. This may be a fitting moment

for recording the tribute of Mr. Macdonald,
the administrator of the *Times* Fund, who wrote
of her before his return to England :—

" Wherever there is disease in its most dangerous form, and the hand of the spoiler distressingly
nigh, there is that incomparable woman sure to
be seen ; her benignant presence is an influence
for good comfort, even among the struggles of
expiring nature. She is a 'ministering angel,'
without any exaggeration, in these hospitals,
and, as her slender form glides quietly along
each corridor, every poor fellow's face softens
with gratitude at the sight of her. When all
the medical officers have retired for the night,
and silence and darkness have settled down upon
those miles of prostrate sick, she may be observed
alone, with a little lamp in her hand, making
her solitary rounds. The popular instinct was
not mistaken, which, when she had set out from
England on her mission of mercy, hailed her as
a heroine ; I trust she may not earn her title
to a higher though sadder appellation. No one
who has observed her fragile figure and delicate

health can avoid misgivings lest these should
fail. With the heart of a true woman, and the
manners of a lady, accomplished and refined
beyond most of her sex, she combines a surprising calmness of judgment and promptitude and
decision of character."

The soldier who watched for her coming,
night by night, on her quiet rounds, after dark,
when other nurses were by her orders resting,
and who only knew her as "the Lady with the
Lamp," has been quoted all over the world ; but
it has been well said that she was also "the lady
with the brain." Hercules had not so big a
task before him when he cleansed the Augean
stables, and the swiftness with which order and
comfort were created in this "hell" of suffering
—for so it has been named by those who saw
and knew—might well be called one of the
wonders of the world.

The secret lay partly in the fact that Florence
Nightingale's whole life had been an offering and
a preparation. She knew all it had been possible
for her to learn of hospital management and

training. She never wasted words, nor frittered away her power. Her authority grew daily. Mr. Herbert's support, even at so great a distance, was, of course, beyond price. Lord Raglan soon found the value of her letters. She inspired her orderlies with utmost devotion, and it is needless to speak of what her patients themselves felt to her. Kinglake is not, like the present writer, a woman, and therefore he can write with a good grace and from his own knowledge what might come with an ill grace from a woman's pen. He shall again therefore be quoted, word for word, through a few pages.

" The growth of her dominion was rapid, was natural, and not unlike the development of what men call 'responsible government.' One of others accepting a task ostensibly subordinate and humble, she yet could not, if she would, divest herself of the authority that belonged to her as a gentlewoman—as a gentlewoman abounding in all the natural gifts, and all the peculiar knowledge required for hospital management. Charged to be in the wards, to smooth the sufferer's pillow, to give him his food and his medicine as ordered by the medical officers, she could not but speak with cogency of the state of the air which she herself had to breathe; she could not be bidden to acquiesce if the beds she approached were impure ; she could scarcely be held to silence if the diet she had been told to administer were not forthcoming ; and, whatever her orders, she could hardly be expected to give a sufferer food which she perceived to be bad or unfit. If the males * did not quite understand the peculiar contrivances fitted for the preparation of hospital diet, might she not, perhaps, disclose her own knowledge, and show them what to do ? Or, if they could not be taught, or imagined that they had not the power to do what was needed, might not she herself compass her object by using the resources which she had at command ? Might not she herself found and organize the requisite kitchens, when she knew that the difference between fit and unfit food was one of life and death to the soldier ? And again, if she chose, might she

* Kinglake's "Invasion of the Crimea," vol. vi. p. 426.

"A Mission of Mercy." Florence Nightingale at Scutari.

(*After the painting by J. Barratt.*)

not expend her own resources in striving against
the foul poisons that surrounded our prostrate
soldiery ?   Rather, far, than that even one man
should suffer from those cruel wants which she
generously chose to supply, it was well that the
State should be humbled, and submit to the taunt
which accused it of taking alms from her hand.

" If we learnt that the cause of the evils afflicting our Levantine hospitals was a want of
impelling and of governing power, we now see
how the want was supplied.   In the absence
of all constituted authority proving equal to the
emergency, there was need—dire need—of a
firm, well-intentioned usurper ;   but amongst the
males acting at Scutari there was no one with
that resolute will, overstriding law, habit, and
custom, which the cruel occasion required ;   for
even Dr. M'Gregor, whose zeal and abilities
were admirable, omitted to lay hold, dictatorially,
of that commanding authority which—because
his chief could not wield it—had fallen into
abeyance.   The will of the males was always
to go on performing their accustomed duties
industriously, steadily, faithfully, each labouring

to the utmost, and, if need be, even to death (as too often, indeed, was the case), in that groove-going 'state of life to which it had pleased God to call him.' The will of the woman, whilst stronger, flew also more straight to the end ; * for what she almost fiercely sought was—not to make good mere equations between official codes of duty and official acts of obedience, but —overcoming all obstacles, to succour, to save our prostrate soldiery, and turn into a well-ordered hospital the hell—the appalling hell—of the vast barrack wards and corridors. Nature seemed, as it were, to ordain that in such a conjuncture the all-essential power which our cramped, over-disciplined males had chosen to leave unexerted should pass to one who would seize it, should pass to one who could wield it—should pass to the Lady-in-Chief.

"To have power was an essential condition of success in her sacred cause ; and of power accordingly she knew and felt the worth, rightly judging that, in all sorts of matters within what she deemed its true range, her word must be law.

* Kinglake's "Invasion of the Crimea," vol. vi.

Like other dictators, she had cast upon her one duty which no one can hope to perform without exciting cavil. For the sake of the cause, she had to maintain her dictatorship, and (on pain of seeing her efforts defeated by anarchical action) to check the growth of authority—of authority in even small matters—if not derived from herself. She was apparently careful in this direction; and, though outwardly calm when provoked, could give strong effect to her anger. On the other hand, when seeing merit in the labours of others, she was ready with generous praise. It was hardly in the nature of things that her sway should excite no jealousies, or that always, hand in hand with the energy which made her great enterprise possible, there should be the cold, accurate justice at which the slower sex aims; but she reigned—painful, heart-rending empire—in a spirit of thorough devotion to the objects of her care, and, upon the whole, with excellent wisdom.

" To all the other sources of power which we have seen her commanding, she added one of a kind less dependent upon her personal qualities. Know-

ing thoroughly the wants of a hospital, and foreseeing, apparently, that the State might fail to meet
them, she had taken care to provide herself with
vast quantities of hospital stores, and by drawing
upon these to make good the shortcoming of any
hampered or lazy official, she not only furnished
our soldiery with the things they were needing,
but administered to the defaulting administrator
a telling, though silent, rebuke; and it would
seem that under this discipline the groove-going
men winced in agony, for they uttered touching
complaints, declaring that the Lady-in-Chief did
not choose to give them time (it was always
time that the males wanted), and that the
moment a want declared itself she made haste
to supply it herself."

Another able writer—a woman—has said that
for Miss Nightingale the testing moment of her
life met her with the coming of the wagon-loads
of wounded men from the battlefield of Inkermann, who were poured into the hospital at
Scutari within twenty-four hours of her arrival.
Had the sight of all that agony and of the sense-

less confusion that received it, led the Lady-in-Chief and her nurses to waste their power in rushing hither and thither in disorganized fear of defeat, their very sympathy and emotion dimming their foresight and clouding their brain, the whole story might have been different. But Miss Nightingale was of those who, by a steadfast obedience hour by hour to the voice within, have attained through the long years to a fine mastery of every nerve and muscle of that frail house wherein they dwell. The more critical the occasion, the more her will rose to meet it. She knew she must think of the welfare, not of one, but of thousands; and for tens of thousands she wrought the change from this welter of misery and death to that clean orderliness which for the moment seemed as far away as the unseen heaven. There were many other faithful and devoted nurses in the Crimea, though few, perhaps, so highly skilled; but her name stands alone as that of the high-hearted and daring spirit who made bold to change the evil system of the past when no man else had done anything but either consent to it or bemoan it. She, at least, had never been bound by red tape, and her whole soul rose up in arms at sight of the awful suffering which had been allowed under the shelter of dogged routine.

Before ten days had passed, she had her kitchen ready and was feeding 800 men every day with well-cooked food, and this in spite of the unforeseen and overwhelming numbers in which the new patients had been poured into the hospitals after Balaclava and Inkermann. She had brought out with her, in the *Vectis*, stores of invalid food, and all sorts of little delicacies surprised the eyes and lips of the hitherto half-starved men. Their gentle nurses brought them beef tea, chicken broth, jelly. They were weak and in great pain, and may be forgiven if their gratitude was, as we are told, often choked with sobs.

Mrs. Tooley tells us of one Crimean veteran, that when he received a basin of arrowroot on his first arrival at the hospital early in the morning, he said to himself, " ' Tommy, me boy, that's all you'll get into your inside this blessed day, and think yourself lucky you've got that.' But two hours later, if another of them blessed angels

didn't come entreating of me to have just a little
chicken broth! Well, I took that, thinking
maybe it was early dinner, and before I had well
done wondering what would happen next, round
the nurse came again with a bit o' jelly; and all
day long at intervals they kept on bringing me
what they called 'a little nourishment.' In the
evening, Miss Nightingale she came and had a
look at me, and says she, 'I hope you're feeling
better?' I could have said, 'Ma'am, I feels as
fit as a fightin' cock,' but I managed to git out
somethin' a bit more polite." *

The barracks had thirteen "coppers," and in
the old days meat and vegetables had just been
tossed into these and boiled together anyhow.
It is easy to imagine the greasy mess to which
the fevered invalids must have been treated by
the time the stuff had been carried round to the
hospital.

But now, sometimes in a single day, thirteen
gallons of chicken broth, and forty gallons of
arrowroot found their way from the new kitchen
to the hospital wards.

* "The Life of Florence Nightingale," by Sarah Tooley.

CHAPTER XIII.

The horrors of Scutari—The victory of the Lady-in-Chief—The Queen's letter—Her gift of butter and treacle.

MISS NIGHTINGALE's discipline was strict; she did not mind the name of autocrat when men were dying by twenties for lack of what only an autocrat could do ; and when there was continual loss of life for want of fitting nourishment, though there had been supplies sent out, as had been said " by the ton-weight," she herself on at least one occasion, broke open the stores and fed her famishing patients. It is true that the ordinary matron would have been dismissed for doing so ; she was not an ordinary matron—she was the Lady-in-Chief. To her that hath shall be given. She had grudged nothing to the service to which from childhood she had given herself—not strength, nor time, nor any other good gift of her womanhood, and having done

her part nobly, fortune aided her. Her friends
were among the " powers that be," and even her
wealth was, in this particular battle, a very
important means of victory. Her beauty would
have done little for her if she had been incompetent, but being to the last degree efficient,
her loveliness gave the final touch to her power
—her loveliness and that personal magnetism
which gave her sway over the hearts and minds
of men, and also, let it be added, of women.
Not only did those in authority give to her of
their best—their best knowledge, their closest
attention, their most untiring service—but she
knew how to discern the true from the false,
and to put to the best use the valuable information
often confided to her. She had many helpers.
Besides her thirty-eight nurses and the chaplain,
Mr. Sidney Osborne, there were her friends,
Mr. and Mrs. Bracebridge, and that splendid
" fag," as he called himself, the young " Mr.
Stafford,"* who had left the gaieties of London
to fetch and carry for the Lady-in-Chief, and—
to quote Mrs. Tooley, " did anything and every-

* Stafford O'Brien.

thing which a handy and gallant gentleman could do to make himself useful to the lady whom he felt honoured to serve." Among those who were most thoughtful in their little gifts for the wounded officers was the wife of our ambassador, Lady Stratford de Redcliffe, and her "beauteous guest," as Kinglake calls her, Lady George Paget. But Miss Nightingale's chief anxiety was not for the officers—they, like herself, had many influences in their favour—her thought was for the nameless rank and file, who had neither money nor rank, and were too often, as she knew, the forgotten pawns on the big chessboard. It was said "she thought only of the men;" she understood well that for their commanders her thought was less needed.

"In the hearts of thousands and thousands of our people," says Kinglake, "there was a yearning to be able to share the toil, the distress, the danger of battling for our sick and wounded troops against the sea of miseries that encompassed them on their hospital pallets; and men still remember how graciously, how simply, how naturally, if so one may speak, the ambassadress

Lady Stratford de Redcliffe and her beauteous guest gave their energies and their time to the work; still remember the generous exertions of Mr. Sidney Osborne and Mr. Joscelyne Percy; still remember, too, how Mr. Stafford— I would rather call him 'Stafford O'Brien'— the cherished yet unspoilt favourite of English society, devoted himself heart and soul to the task of helping and comforting our prostrate soldiery in the most frightful depths of their misery.

"Many found themselves embarrassed when trying to choose the best direction they could for their generous impulses; and not, I think, the least praiseworthy of all the self-sacrificing enterprises which imagination devised was that of the enthusiastic young fellow who, abandoning his life of ease, pleasure, and luxury, went out, as he probably phrased it, to 'fag' for the Lady-in-Chief. Whether fetching and carrying for her, or writing for her letters or orders, or orally conveying her wishes to public servants or others, he, for months and months, faithfully toiled, obeying in all things her word.

"There was grace—grace almost mediæval—
in his simple yet romantic idea ; and, if humbly,
still not the less usefully he aided the sacred
cause, for it was one largely, mainly dependent
on the power of the lady he served ; so that,
when by obeying her orders he augmented her
means of action, and saved her precious time,
there were unnumbered sufferers deriving sure
benefit from his opportune, well-applied help.
By no other kind of toil, however ambitiously
aimed, could he well have achieved so much
good."

But there was many a disappointment, much
that did not seem "good luck" by any means,
and that called for great courage and endurance.
The stores, which Mr. Herbert had sent out in
such abundance, had gone to Varna by mistake,
and the loss of the *Prince*, a ship laden with
ample supplies, a fortnight after Miss Nightingale's arrival, was a very serious matter.

Warm clothing for the frost-bitten men brought
in from Sebastopol was so badly needed that one
nurse, writing home, told her people : "When-

ever a man opens his mouth with 'Please, ma'am, I want to speak to you,' my heart sinks within me, for I feel sure it will end in flannel shirts."

Every one had for too long been saying "all right," when, as a matter of fact, it was all wrong. Here once again it is best to quote Kinglake. "By shunning the irksome light," he says, "by choosing a low standard of excellence, and by vaguely thinking 'War' an excuse for defects which war did not cause, men, it seems, had contrived to be satisfied with the condition of our hospitals; but the Lady-in-Chief was one who would harbour no such content, seek no such refuge from pain. Not for her was the bliss — fragile bliss — of dwelling in any false paradise. She confronted the hideous truth. Her first care was—Eve-like—to dare to know, and—still Eve-like—to force dreaded knowledge on the faltering lord of creation. Then declaring against acquiescence in horror and misery which firmness and toil might remove, she waged her ceaseless war against custom and sloth, gaining every day on the enemy, and achieving, as we saw, in December, that which to eyes less intent than her own upon actual saving of life, and actual restoration of health, seemed already the highest excellence."

But, of course, what most made the men adore her was her loving individual care for each of those for whom she felt herself responsible. There was one occasion on which she begged to be allowed to try whether she could nurse back to possible life five wounded men who were being given up as "hopeless cases," and did actually succeed in doing so.

In all that terrible confusion of suffering that surrounded her soon after her first arrival, the first duty of the doctors was to sort out from the wounded as they arrived those cases which they could help and save from those which it seemed no human surgery could help.

While this was being done she stood by : she never spared herself the sight of suffering, and her eyes—the trained eyes that had all the intuition of a born nurse—saw a glimmer of hope for five badly wounded men who were being set aside among those for whom nothing could be done.

"Will you give me those five men?" she asked. She knew how much might be done by gentle and gradual feeding, and by all the intently watchful care of a good nurse, to give them just enough strength to risk the surgery that might save them. With her own hand, spoonful by spoonful, as they were able to bear it, she gave the nourishment, and by her own night-long watching and tending in the care of all those details which to a poor helpless patient may make the difference between life and death —the purifying of the air, the avoidance of draughts, the mending of the fire—she nursed her five patients back into a condition in which the risks of an operation were, to say the least of it, greatly lessened. The operation was in each case successfully performed; by all human standards it may be said that she saved the lives of all the five.

She never spared herself, though she sometimes spared others. She has been known to stand for twenty hours out of the twenty-four, and at night, when she had sent her day-nurses to rest, it was she herself who watched in all the wards and silently cared for the needs of one and another. Is it any wonder that " there was worship almost in the gratitude of the prostrate sufferer, who saw her glide into his ward, and at last approach his bedside ?   The magic of her power over men used often to be felt in the room—the dreaded, the blood-stained room——where ' operations ' took place.   There, perhaps, the maimed soldier, if not yet resigned to his fate, might at first be craving death rather than meet the knife of the surgeon ; but, when such a one looked and saw that the honoured Lady-in-Chief was patiently standing beside him, and—with lips closely set and hands folded—decreeing herself to go through the pain of witnessing pain, he used to fall into the mood for obeying her silent command, and —finding strange support in her presence—bring himself to submit and endure." *

M. Soyer, who placed his culinary art at her service, has written a book about his experiences in which he tells us that, after a merry evening in the doctors' quarters, when on his way back to his own, he saw by a faint light a little group

* Kinglake's "Invasion of Crimea."

—shadowy in the half-darkness—in a corner of one of the corridors. A Sister stood beside Miss Nightingale with a lighted candle that she might see clearly enough to scribble down the last wishes of the dying soldier who was supported on the bed beside her. With its deep colouring, described as like a grave study by Rembrandt, the little picture drew the passer-by, and for a few minutes he watched unseen while the Lady-in-Chief took into those "tender womanly hands" the watch and trinkets of the soldier, who with his last gasping breath was trying to make clear to her his farewell message to his wife and children. And this seems to have been but one among many kindred scenes.

We have all heard of the man who watched till her shadow fell across the wall by his bed that he might at least kiss that shadow as it passed ; but few of us, perhaps, know the whole story. The man was a Highland soldier who had been doomed to lose his arm by amputation. Miss Nightingale believed that she might possibly be able to save the arm by careful nursing, and she begged that she might at least be allowed to try. Nursing was to her an art as well as a labour of love. The ceaseless care in matters of detail, which she considered the very alphabet of that art, stand out clearly in her own *Notes on Nursing*. And in this instance her skill and watchfulness and untiring effort saved the man's arm. No wonder that he wanted to kiss her shadow!

To the wives of the soldiers she was indeed a saving angel. When she arrived at Scutari, they were living, we are told, literally in holes and corners of the hospital. Their clothes were worn out. They had neither bonnets, nor shoes, nor any claim on rations. Poor faithful creatures, many of them described in the biographies as respectable and decent, they had followed their husbands through all the horrors of the campaign, and now, divided from them and thrust aside for want of space, they were indeed in sorry case.

Well might Miss Nightingale write later, and well may we all lay it to heart—" When the improvements in our system are discussed, let not the wife and child of the soldier be forgotten."

After being moved about from one den to

another, the poor women—some wives and some, alas, widows—had been quartered in a few damp rooms in the hospital basement, where those who wanted solitude or privacy could do nothing to secure it beyond hanging a few rags on a line as a sort of screen between home and home. And in these desolate quarters many babies had been born.

It was but the last drop of misery in their cup when, early in 1855, a month or two after Miss Nightingale's arrival, a drain broke in the basement, and fever followed.

Miss Nightingale had already sought them out, and from her own stores given them food and clothing; but now she did not rest until through her influence a house had been requisitioned and cleaned and furnished for them out of her own funds. Next, after fitting out the widows to return to their homes, employment was found for the wives who remained. Work was found for some of them in Constantinople, but for most of them occupation was at hand in the laundry she had set going, and there those who were willing to do their part could earn from 10s. to 14s. a week. In this way, through our heroine's wise energy, helped by the wife and daughter of Dr. Blackwood, one of the army chaplains, we are told that about 500 women were cared for.

There had already arrived through the hands of Mr. Sidney Herbert, who forwarded it to Miss Nightingale, a message from Queen Victoria— in effect a letter—which greatly cheered the army and also strengthened Miss Nightingale's position.

"WINDSOR CASTLE,
"*December* 6, '54.

"Would you tell Mrs. Herbert," wrote the Queen to Mr. Sidney Herbert, "that I beg she would let me see frequently the accounts she receives from Miss Nightingale or Mrs. Brace-bridge, as I hear no details of the wounded, though I see so many from officers, etc., about the battlefield, and naturally the former must interest me more than any one.

"Let Mrs. Herbert also know that I wish Miss Nightingale and the ladies would tell these poor, noble wounded and sick men that no one takes a warmer interest or feels more for their sufferings or admires their courage and heroism more than their Queen.   Day and night she thinks of her beloved troops.   So does the Prince.

" Beg Mrs. Herbert to communicate these my words to those ladies, as I know that our sympathy is much valued by these noble fellows.

" VICTORIA."

Miss Nightingale agreed with the Queen in her use of the word "noble" here, for she herself has written of the men :—

" Never came from any of them one word nor one look which a gentleman would not have used ; and while paying this humble tribute to humble courtesy, the tears come into my eyes as I think how, amidst scenes of . . . loathsome disease and death, there rose above it all the innate dignity, gentleness, and chivalry of the men (for never, surely, was chivalry so strikingly exemplified), shining in the midst of what must be considered as the lowest sinks of human misery, and preventing instinctively the use of one expression which could distress a gentlewoman."

Having transcribed the Queen's letter, this
may be a good place for adding from the letters
of Sister Aloysius a little instance of Her
Majesty's homely kindness to her troops whenever she heard of any need which she could
supply :—

"When Miss Stanley reached England, Her
Majesty the Queen (anxious, of course, to hear
all about her soldiers) sent for her ; and when
the interview was nearly over Her Majesty asked
her what she thought the poor soldiers would
like—she was anxious to send them a present.
Miss Stanley said : 'Oh, I do know what they
would like—plenty of flannel shirts, mufflers,
butter, and treacle.' Her Majesty said they must
have all these things ; and they did come out
in abundance : Kullali got its share of the gifts.
But the very name of butter or treacle was
enough for the doctors : they said they would
not allow it into the wards, because it would be
going about in bits of paper and daubing everything. So Rev. Mother at once interposed, and
said if the doctors allowed it, she would have it

distributed in a way that could give no trouble. They apologized, and said they should have known that, and at once left everything to her. Each Sister got her portion of butter and treacle (which were given only to the convalescent patients), and when the bell rang every evening for tea she stood at the table in the centre of the ward, and each soldier walked over and got his bread buttered, and some treacle if he wished spread on like jam. We told them it was a gift from the Queen ; and if Her Majesty could only have seen how gratified they were it would have given her pleasure. One evening Lady Stratford, and some distinguished guests who were staying at the Embassy, came, and were much pleased to see how happy and comfortable the men were, and how much they enjoyed Her Majesty's gifts."

CHAPTER XIV.

Miss Nightingale's saving sense of humour gleams forth in her letters in the most delightful way, even in the darkest days. In the following, something of the hugeness of her task is dimly seen through the comic background of the unbecoming cap that "If I'd known, ma'am, I wouldn't have come, ma'am." Here is the letter just as it is given in Lord Herbert's life. It begins abruptly, evidently quoting from a conversation just held with one of the staff nurses :—

"'I came out, ma'am, prepared to submit to everything, to be put upon in every way. But there are some things, ma'am, one can't submit to. There is the caps, ma'am, that suits one

face and some that suits another.; and if I'd
known, ma'am, about the caps, great as was my
desire to come out to nurse at Scutari, I wouldn't
have come, ma'am.'—*Speech of Mrs. L., Barrack
Hospital, Scutari, Asiatic Side, November* 14, 1854.

"Time must be at a discount with the man
who can adjust the balance of such an important
question as the above, and I for one have none,
as you will easily suppose when I tell you that
on Thursday last we had 1,175 sick and wounded
in this hospital (among whom 120 cholera patients), and 650 severely wounded in the other
building, called the General Hospital, of which
we also have charge, when a message came to
me to prepare for 510 wounded on our side of
the hospital, who were arriving from the dreadful affair of November 5, from Balaclava, in
which battle were 1,763 wounded and 442
killed, besides 96 officers wounded and 38 killed.
I always expected to end my days as a hospital
matron, but I never expected to be barrack mistress.   We had but half an hour's notice before
they began landing the wounded.   Between one
and nine o'clock we had the mattresses stuffed,

sewn up, laid down (alas! only upon matting on the floor), the men washed and put to bed, and all their wounds dressed.

"We are very lucky in our medical heads. Two of them are brutes and four are angels—for this is a work which makes either angels or devils of men, and of women too. As for the assistants, they are all cubs, and will, while a man is breathing his last breath under the knife, lament the 'annoyance of being called up from their dinners by such a fresh influx of wounded.' But unlicked cubs grow up into good old bears, though I don't know how; for certain it is, the old bears are good. We have now four miles of beds and not eighteen inches apart.

"We have our quarters in one tower of the barracks, and all this fresh influx has been laid down between us and the main guard, in two corridors, with a line of beds down each side, just room for one person to pass between, and four wards. Yet in the midst of this appalling horror (we are steeped up to our necks in blood) there is good—and I can truly say, like St.

Peter, 'It is good for us to be here'—though
I doubt whether, if St. Peter had been there,
he would have said so."

Meanwhile England, stirred to its depths by
the accounts given by Mr. William Howard
Russell, of the sufferings of our soldiers, had
begged the *Times*, in whose pages his letters
appeared, to receive funds and send them out
by the hand of Mr. Macdonald, a man of vigour,
firmness, and good sense, and "loyally devoted
to his duty." Before leaving England, he saw
the Inspector-General of the army, Dr. Andrew
Smith, and also the Duke of Newcastle, but was
assured that Government had already provided
so amply for the sick and wounded that his fund
was not likely to be needed. When he reached
the Bosphorus all the official people there talked
to him in the same strain. But there leaked
out through an officer on duty one little fact
that showed how much such assurances were
worth.

It seemed that the 39th Regiment was actually
on its way to the severities of a Crimean winter

with only the light summer clothing that would be worn in hot countries. Happily, the surgeon of the regiment appealed to Mr. Macdonald, and, more happily still, Mr. Macdonald dared to go beyond his exact instructions and give help out of his fund which might prevent illness, instead of waiting for the moment when death was already at the door. He went into the markets of Constantinople and bought then and there a suit of flannels or other woollens for every man in that regiment.

Mr. Macdonald saw that he must be ready to offer help, or red tape and loyalty together would seal the lips of men in the service, lest they should seem to be casting a slur on the army administration.

There is humour of the grimmest kind in what resulted. The chief of the Scutari hospitals told him " nothing was wanted," and on pushing his inquiry with a yet more distinguished personage, he was actually advised to spend the money on building a church at Pera !

" Yet at that very time," says Kinglake,

"wants so dire as to include want of hospital furniture and of shirts for the patients, and of the commonest means for obtaining cleanliness, were afflicting our stricken soldiery in the hospitals."

The Pera proposal — rightly described as "astounding"—led to an interview with the Lady-in-Chief. Tears and laughter must have met in her heart as she heard this absurdity, and away she took him—money as well—to the very centre of her commissariat, to see for himself the daily demands and the gaping need —furniture, pillows, sheets, shirts—endless appliances and drugs—that need seemed truly endless, and many hours daily he spent with her in the Nurses' Tower, taking down lists of orders for the storekeepers in Constantinople. Here was the right help at last—not pretty mufflers for men in need of shirts, nor fine cambric for stout bed-linen.

However, from the Lady-in-Chief Mr. Macdonald soon learned the truth, and the course he then took was one of the simplest kind, but it

worked a mighty change. He bought the
things needed, and the authorities, succumbing
at last to this excruciating form of demonstra-
tion, had to witness the supply of wants which
before they had refused to confess. So now,
besides using the stores which she had at her own
command, the Lady-in-Chief could impart wants
felt in our hospitals to Mr. Macdonald with the
certainty that he would hasten to meet them by
applying what was called the " *Times* Fund " in
purchasing the articles needed.

"It was thus," adds Kinglake, "that under
the sway of motives superbly exalted, a great
lady came to the rescue of our prostrate soldiery,
made good the default of the State, won the
gratitude, the rapt admiration of an enthusiastic
people, and earned for the name she bears a pure,
a lasting renown.

"She even did more. By the very power
of her fame, but also, I believe, by the wisdom
and the authority of her counsels, she founded,
if so one may speak, a gracious dynasty that
still reigns supreme in the wards where sufferers

lie, and even brings solace, brings guidance, brings hope, into those dens of misery that, until the blessing has reached them, seem only to harbour despair. When into the midst of such scenes the young high-bred lady now glides, she wears that same sacred armour—the gentle attire of the servitress—which seemed ' heavenly ' in the eyes of our soldiers at the time of the war, and finds strength to meet her dire task, because she knows by tradition what the first of the dynasty proved able to confront and to vanquish in the wards of the great Barrack Hospital."

In everything a woman's hand and brain had been needed. It was, for instance, of little use to receive in the evening, after barrack fires were out, food which had been asked for from the supplies for some meal several hours earlier ; yet that, it appears, was the sort of thing that happened. And too much of the food officially provided, even when it did reach the patients at last, had been unfit for use.

As for the question of laundry, a washing contract that had only succeeded in washing seven shirts for two or three thousand men could not have been permitted to exist under any feminine management. Nor could any trained or knowledgeable nurse have allowed for a single day the washing of infectious bed-linen in one common tub with the rest. Yet this had been the condition of affairs before the Lady-in-Chief came on the scenes. In speaking of her work among the soldiers' wives it has already been noted how she quickly hired and fitted up a house close to the hospital as a laundry, where under sanitary regulations 500 shirts and 150 other articles were washed every week.

Then there arose the practical question of what could be done for the poor fellows who had no clothes at all except the grimy and blood-stained garments in which they arrived, and we are told that in the first three months, out of her own private funds, she provided the men with ten thousand shirts.

The drugs had all been in such confusion that once when Mrs. Bracebridge had asked three times for chloride of lime and been assured that there was none, Miss Nightingale insisted on a thorough search, and not less than ninety pounds of it were discovered.

The semi-starvation of many hospital patients before Miss Nightingale's arrival, noted on an earlier page, was chiefly the result of mismanagement—mismanagement on the part of those who meant well—often, indeed, meant the very best within their power, but among whom there was, until her coming, no central directing power, with brain and heart alike capable and energizing and alive to all the vital needs of deathly illness —alert with large foreseeing outlook, yet shrewd and swift in detail.

It is at first puzzling to compare Kinglake's picture of the confusion and suffering, even while he is defending Lord Raglan, with some of the letters in Lord Stanmore's " Life of Lord Herbert," especially one from General Estcourt, in which he says " never was an army better fed." But even in this letter—dated, be it noted, a fortnight after Miss Nightingale's arrival—the next sentence, which refers, of course, to the army in general and not to the hospitals under her management, shows the same muddling that had pursued the hospitals until she came to their aid with Mr. Herbert and the War Office at her back; for after saying that the ration is ample and most liberal, it adds—and the italics are mine—"*but the men cannot cook for want of camp-kettles and for want of fuel.*"

Yet even with regard to the hospitals, it is startling to find Mr. Bracebridge, in his first letter to Mr. Herbert, speaking of the Barrack Hospital as clean and airy. But people have such odd ideas of what is " clean and airy," and it would seem that he thought it " clean and airy " for the patients to have no proper arrangements for washing, for the drains to be in such a noisome state as to need engineering, and for six dead dogs to be rotting under the windows ! I suppose he liked the look of the walls and the height of the ceilings, and wanted, moreover, to comfort Mr. Herbert's sad heart at a time when all England was up in arms at the mistakes made in transport and other arrangements.

The letters of the chaplain to Mr. Herbert are full of interest, and in reading the following we have to put ourselves back into the mind of a time that looked anxiously to see whether Miss Nightingale was really equal to her task— an idea which to us of to-day seems foolish and timorous, but which was, after all, quite natural, seeing that she was new and untried in this particular venture of army nursing, and that half the onlookers had no idea of the long and varied training she had had.

" MY DEAR HERBERT,—I have now had near a week's opportunity of closely observing the details of the hospitals at Scutari. First, as to Miss Nightingale and her company, nothing can be said too strong in their praise ; she works them wonderfully, and they are so useful that I have no hesitation in saying some twenty more of the same sort would be a very great blessing to the establishment. Her nerve is equal to her good sense ; she, with one of her nurses and myself, gave efficient aid at an amputation of the thigh yesterday. She was just as cool as if she had had to do it herself. We are close allies, and through Macdonald and the funds at my own command, I get her everything for which she asks, and this is saying a great deal.

"My honest view of the matter is this : I found but too great evidence of the staff and means being unequal to the emergency ; the requirements have almost doubled through the last two unhappy actions at Balaclava. Still, day by day I see manifest improvement ; no government, no nation could have provided, on a sudden, staff and appliances for accident wards miles in length, and for such sickness as that horrid Varna dysentery. To manage more than three thousand casualties of the worst nature is indeed a task to be met in an entirely satisfactory way by nothing short of a miraculous energy with the means it would require. The men are landed necessarily in a most pitiable state, and have to be carried up steep ground for considerable distance, either by those beasts of Turks, who are as stupid as callous, or by our invalids, who are not equal to the task. Still, it is done, and as this is war, not peace, and Scutari is really a battlefield, I am more disposed to lament than to blame.

"There seems now, so far as I can see, no lack of lint and plaister ; there is a lack of linen, —we have sent home for it.   The surgeons are working their utmost, and serious cases seem treated with great humanity and skill.   There was and is an awful want of shirts for the men, and socks, and such matters ; we have already let Miss Nightingale have all she applies for, and this morning I, with Macdonald's sanction, or, rather, in concert with him, have sent to the Crimea a large stock of shirts of warm serge, socks, flannel, tea, etc., etc.   I spend the best part of every day there acting, at one time as priest to the dying, at another helping the surgeons or the men to dress their wounds ; again, I go to the landing-place and try to work them into method for an hour or two, etc., etc.   One and all are now most kind and civil to me, meet my wishes in every way they can.   Alas ! I fear, with every possible effort of the existing establishment, the crisis is still too great ; there are wanting hundreds of beds—that is, many hundreds have only matting between the beds and the stone floor.   I slept here Sunday night, and

walked the wards late and early in the morning ;
I fear the cold weather in these passages will
produce on men so crippled and so maimed
much supplementary evil in the way of coughs
and chest diseases. The wounded do better than
the sick. I scarce pray with one of the latter
one day but I hear he is dead on the morrow.
. . . I am glad to say the authorities have left
off swearing they had everything and wanted
nothing ; they are now grateful for the help
which, with the fund at command, we liberally
meet. The wounds are, many of them, of the
most fearful character, and yet I have not heard
a murmur, even from those who, from the pressing urgency of the case, are often left with most
obvious grounds of complaint. Stafford O'Brien
is here ; he, at my suggestion, aids my son and
self in letter writing for the poor creatures. My
room is a post office ; I pay the post of every
letter from every hospital patient, and we write
masses every day. They show one what the
British soldier really is ; I only wish to God the
people of England, who regard the red coat as a
mere guise of a roystering rake in the private and

a dandified exclusive in the officer, could see the patience, true modesty, and courageous endurance of all ranks.

"Understand me clearly. I could pick many a hole; I could show where head has been wanting, truth perverted, duty neglected, etc.; but I feel that the pressure was such and of so frightful, so severe (in one way) a character, there is such an effort at what we desire, that I for one cry out of the past '*non mi ricordo;*' of the present, 'If the cart is in the rut, there is every shoulder at the wheel.' The things wanted we cannot wait for you to supply, in England; if the slaughter is to go on as it has done the last fortnight, the need must be met at once. Macdonald is doing his work most sensibly, steadily, and I believe not only with no offence to any, but is earning the goodwill of all."

Truth is a two-edged sword, and for purposes of rebuke or reform Miss Nightingale used it at times with keenness and daring. In that sense this glowing, loving-hearted woman knew how on occasions to be stern. Her salt never

lost its savour.   She was swift, efficient, capable
to the last degree, and she was also high-spirited
and sometimes sharp-tongued.   Perhaps we love
her all the more for being so human.   A person
outwardly all perfection, if not altogether divine,
is apt to give the idea that there are faults hidden
up somewhere.   It was not so with Miss Nightingale.   Her determination to carry at all costs
the purpose she had in hand laid her often open
to criticism, for, just as she was ready on occasion
to override her own feelings, so also she was ready
sometimes to override the feelings of others.   Mr.
Herbert judged from her letters that an addition
to her staff of nurses would be welcome, but we
saw that when the new band of forty-six arrived,
under the escort of Miss Nightingale's old friend
Miss Stanley, they were not admitted to the
hospital at Scutari, and to tell the truth, Miss
Nightingale was very angry at their being thrust
upon her, just when she was finding her own
staff rather a " handful."   In point of fact, she
not only wrote a very warm letter to her old
friend Mr. Herbert, but she also formally gave
in her resignation.

This was not accepted. Mr. Herbert's generous sweetness of nature, his love for the writer, and his belief that she was the one person needed in the hospitals, and was doing wonders there, led him to write a very noble and humble reply, saying that *he* had made a mistake—which, indeed, was true enough—in taking his well-meant step without consulting her. She yielded her point in so far as to remain at her post, now that Miss Stanley and her staff had moved on to Therapia and Smyrna, and were doing real good there, Miss Stanley having given up all her own plans, to remain and look after the nurses who had come under her escort.

But, apart from the fact that it would have been a great hindrance to discipline to have forty-six women on her hands who had *not* promised obedience to her, as had her own nurses, a little sidelight is thrown upon it all by these words in one of Miss Stanley's own letters, speaking of the nurses under her guardianship :—

" The first night there was great dissatisfaction

among them, and a strong inclination to strike work. 'We are not come out to be cooks, housemaids, and washerwomen,' and they dwelt considerably on Mr. Herbert's words about equality. *They are like troublesome children.*"

Though our sympathy goes out to Miss Stanley, it is not impossible that Miss Nightingale's decision may have saved Scutari from unavoidable confusions of authority which would have been very unseemly, and from more than a possibility of defeat in the experiment she was making, in the eyes of all Europe, as to how far women could be wisely admitted into military hospitals. Such confusion might have arisen, not from any fault in Miss Nightingale or Miss Stanley, but from the special work of reorganization which had to be done at Scutari, and the special code of obedience by which Miss Nightingale's staff had been prepared for it. She did not want for such work any " troublesome children."

CHAPTER XV.

MEANWHILE Miss Stanley's letters give us a very interesting informal glimpse of the work that was going on and of Miss Nightingale herself. Here is one in which she describes her visit to her in the hospital at Scutari :—

"We passed down two or three of these immense corridors, asking our way as we went. At last we came to the guard-room, another corridor, then through a door into a large, busy kitchen, where stood Mrs. Margaret Williams, who seemed much pleased to see me : then a heavy curtain was raised ; I went through a door, and there sat dear Flo writing on a small unpainted deal table. I never saw her looking better. She had on her black merino, trimmed with black velvet, clean linen collar and cuffs, apron, white cap with a black handkerchief tied over it; and there was Mrs. Bracebridge, looking so nice, too. I was quite satisfied with my welcome. It was settled at once that I was to sleep here, especially as, being post day, Flo could not attend to me till the afternoon.

"The sofa is covered with newspapers just come in by the post. I have been sitting for an hour here, having some coffee, and writing, Mrs. Clarke coming in to see what I have wanted, in spite of what I could say.

"The work this morning was the sending off General Adams's remains, and the arrangements consequent upon it.

"A stream of people every minute.

"'Please, ma'am, have you any black-edged paper?'

"'Please, what can I give which would keep on his stomach; is there any arrowroot to-day for him?'

"'No; the tubs of arrowroot must be for the worst cases; we cannot spare him any, nor is there any jelly to-day ; try him with some eggs, etc.'

" ' Please, Mr. Gordon wishes to see Miss Nightingale about the orders she gave him.'

" Mr. Sabine comes in for something else.

" Mr. Bracebridge in and out about General Adams, and orders of various kinds."

Such was the busy life of which Miss Nightingale was the queen, though, unlike the queen-bee of the ordinary honey-hive, this queen of nurses was the hardest-worked and most severely strained worker in the whole toiling community.

It was early in the spring of 1855 that in the feeding department, which she rightly considered of great importance to her invalids, she received unexpected help.

This came from M. Soyer, who may be remembered by more than one old Londoner as at one time *chef* of the New Reform Club, where his biography, which contains some interesting illustrations, still adorns the library. M. Soyer begged to be allowed the command of the hospital kitchen at Scutari. He was an expert and an enthusiast, and very amusing.

Also what he offered was of no slight importance and unselfishness. In February, 1855, he wrote as follows to the *Times* :—

"Sir,—After carefully perusing the letter of your correspondent, dated Scutari, in your impression of Wednesday last, I perceive that, although the kitchen under the superintendence of Miss Nightingale affords so much relief, the system of management at the large one at the Barrack Hospital is far from being perfect. I propose offering my services gratuitously, and proceeding direct to Scutari at my own personal expense, to regulate that important department, if the Government will honour me with their confidence, and grant me the full power of acting according to my knowledge and experience in such matters.—I have the honour to remain, sir, your obedient servant, A. SOYER."

His proposal was accepted, and on his arrival at Scutari he was welcomed by Miss Nightingale in what he names, after his rather florid manner, " a sanctuary of benevolence." There he presented his letters and parcels from the Duchess of Sutherland and Mr. Stafford and others, the Duchess especially commending him to the Lady-in-Chief as likely to be of service in the cooking department. He was found to be a most valuable ally, and his letters and writings, since published, are full of interest. He wrote home at once, saying : " I must especially express my gratitude to Miss Nightingale, who from her extraordinary intelligence and the good organization of her kitchen procured me every material for making a commencement, and thus saved me at least one week's sheer loss of time, as my model kitchen did not arrive till Saturday last."

This is interesting, because it shows yet once more Miss Nightingale's thoroughness and foresight and attention to detail—the more valuable in one whose outlook at the same time touched so wide a skyline, and was so large in its noble care for a far-off future and a world of many nations, never bounded by her own small island or her own church pew.

Soyer's description of her is worth giving in full, and later we shall, through his eyes, have a vision of her as she rode to Balaclava.

"Her visage as regards expression is very remarkable, and one can almost anticipate by her countenance what she is about to say : alternately, with matters of the most grave importance, a gentle smile passes radiantly over her countenance, thus proving her evenness of temper ; at other times, when wit or a pleasantry prevails, the heroine is lost in the happy, good-natured smile which pervades her face, and you recognize only the charming woman. Her dress is generally of a greyish or black tint ; she wears a simple white cap, and often a rough apron. In a word, her whole appearance is religiously simple and unsophisticated. In conversation no member of the fair sex can be more amiable and gentle than Miss Nightingale. Removed from her arduous and cavalier-like duties, which require the nerve of a Hercules—and she possesses it when required—she is Rachel on the stage in both tragedy and comedy."

Soyer's help and loyalty proved invaluable all through the campaign. His volume of memories adds a vivid bit of colour here and there to these pages. His own life had been romantic, and he saw everything from the romantic point of view.

We read and know that although Sidney Herbert's letter to Dr. Menzies, the principal medical officer at Scutari, asked that all regard should be paid to every wish of the Lady-in-Chief, and that was in itself a great means of power, the greatest power of all lay in her own personality and its compelling magnetism, which drew others to obedience. The attractive force of a strong, clear, comprehensive mind, and still more of a soul on fire with high purpose and deep compassion, which never wasted themselves in words, became tenfold the more powerful for the restraint and self-discipline which held all boisterous expression of them in check—her word, her very glance,

"Winning its way with extreme gentleness
Through all the outworks of suspicious pride."

Her strength was to be tried to the uttermost ;

for scarcely had her work in the hospital begun when cholera came stalking over the threshold. Day and night among the dying and the dead she and her nurses toiled with fearless devotion, each one carrying her life in her hand, but seldom, indeed, even thinking of that in the heroic struggle to save as many other lives as possible.

Miss Nightingale long afterwards, when talking of services of a far easier kind, once said to a professional friend that no one was fit to be a nurse who did not really enjoy precisely those duties of a sick-room which the ordinary uneducated woman counts revolting ; and if she was, at this time, now and then impatient with stupidity and incompetence and carelessness, that is not wonderful in one whose effort was always at high level, and for whom every detail was of vivid interest, because she realized that often on exactitude in details hung the balance between life and death.

On their first arrival she and her nurses may, no doubt, have had to bear cold-shouldering and jealousy ; but in the long agony of the cholera visitation they were welcomed as veritable angels of light. It would be easy to be sensational in describing the scenes amid which they moved, for before long the hospital was filled, day and night, with two long processions : on one side came in those who carried the sick men in on their stretchers, and on the other side those who carried out the dead. The orderlies could not have been trusted to do the nursing that was required ; the "stuping"—a professional method of wholesale hot fomentations and rubbings to release the iron rigidity of the cholera patient's body—was best done by skilled and gentle hands, and even in *such* hands, so bad were the surrounding conditions—the crowding, the bad drainage, the impure water—that, despite the utmost devotion, only a small proportion of lives could be saved.

It was especially at this time that the feeling towards the Lady-in-Chief deepened into a trust that was almost worship. Watchful, resourceful, unconquered, with a mind that, missing no detail, yet took account of the widest issues and the farthest ends, she was yet full of divine tenderness for each sufferer whom with her own hands she tended; and, although she did not nurse the officers—she left that to others—in her devotion to Tommy Atkins she had been known to be on her feet, as already has been said, for twenty hours on end; and, whether she was kneeling or standing, stooping or lifting, always an ideal nurse.

The graves round the hospitals were not dug deep enough, and the air became even fouler than before. To the inroads of cholera the suffering of Sebastopol patients added a new form of death. . Sister Aloysius writes of these men who came in by scores and hundreds from the trenches, and whom this Sister, greatly valued by the Lady-in-Chief, helped to nurse both at Scutari and at Balaclava :—

" I must say something of my poor frost-bitten patients. The men who came from the 'front,' as they called it, had only thin linen suits, no other clothing to keep out the Crimean frost of 1854–5. When they were carried in on the stretchers which conveyed so many to their last resting-place, their clothes had to be cut off. In most cases the flesh and clothes were frozen together ; and, as for the feet, the boots had to be cut off bit by bit, the flesh coming off with them ; many pieces of the flesh I have seen remain in the boot.

"We have just received some hundreds of poor creatures, worn out with sufferings beyond any you could imagine, in the Crimea, where the cold is so intense that a soldier described to me the Russians and the Allies in a sudden skirmish, and neither party able to draw a trigger ! So fancy what the poor soldiers must endure in the ' trenches.'

"It was a comfort to think that these brave men had some care, all that we could procure for them. For at this time the food was very bad— goat's flesh, and sometimes what they called mutton, but black, blue, and green. Yet who could complain of anything after the sufferings I have faintly described—borne, too, with such patience : not a murmur ! . . . One day, after a batch had arrived from the Crimea, and I had gone my rounds through them, one of my orderlies told me that a man wanted to speak one word to me.

"When I had a moment I went to him. 'Tell me at once what you want; I have worse cases to see after'—he did not happen to be very bad. 'All I want to know, ma'am, is, are you one of our own Sisters of Mercy from Ireland ?' 'Yes,' I said, 'your very own.' 'God be praised for that !'

"Another poor fellow said to me one day, 'Do they give you anything good out here ?' 'Oh yes,' I said; 'why do you ask me ?' 'Because, ma'am, you gave me a piece of chicken for my dinner, and I kept some of it for you.' He pulled it out from under his head and offered it to me. I declined the favour with thanks. I never could say enough of those kind-hearted soldiers and their consideration for us in the midst of their sufferings."

CHAPTER XVI.

ABOUT the middle of December Miss Nightingale had to rebuke very severely one of her own nurses, who had written a letter to the *Times* which made a great sensation by its lurid picture of the evils in the hospital—a misrepresentation so great that the nurse herself confessed in the end that it was "a tissue of exaggerations"—perhaps "inexactitudes" would be our modern word.

Meanwhile, the small-minded parochial gossips at home were wasting their time in discussing Miss Nightingale's religious opinions. One who worked so happily with all who served the same Master was first accused under the old cry of "Popery," and then under the equally silly label of "Unitarianism." Her friend Mrs. Herbert, in rebuking parish gossip, felt it necessary to unpin these two labels and loyally pin on a new one, by explaining that in reality she was rather "Low Church." The really sensible person, with whom, doubtless, Lady Herbert would have fully agreed, was the Irish parson, and his like, when he replied to some foolish questions about her that Miss Nightingale belonged to a very rare sect indeed—the sect of the Good Samaritans.

Miss Stanley tells a most amusing story of how one of the military chaplains complained to Miss Jebbut that very improper books had been circulated in the wards ; she pressed in vain to know what they were. "As I was coming away he begged for five minutes' conversation, said he was answerable for the men and what they read, and he must protest against sentiments he neither approved nor understood, and that he would fetch me the book. It was Keble's 'Christian Year,' which Miss Jebbut had lent to a sick midshipman ! "

It was a brave heart indeed that the Good Samaritan needed now, with cholera added to the other horrors of hospital suffering, and the frost-bitten cases from Sebastopol were almost equally heart-rending.

It was early in January 1855 that Miss Stanley escorted fifty more nurses. Most of them worked under Miss Anderson at the General Hospital at Scutari, but eight were sent into the midst of the fighting at Balaclava, and of the life there "at the front" the letters of Sister Aloysius give a terrible picture. We have, for instance, the story of a man ill and frost-bitten, who found he could not turn on his side because his feet were frozen to those of the soldier opposite. And it came to pass that for two months the death-rate in the hospitals was sixty per cent.

Night after night, the restless, lonely sufferers watched for the coming of the slender, white-capped figure with the little light that she shaded so carefully lest it should waken any sleeper, as she passed through the long corridors watching over the welfare of her patients, and to them she was "the Lady with the Lamp."

We still see with the American poet :—

"The wounded from the battle-plain,
In dreary hospitals of pain,
  The cheerless corridors,
  The cold and stony floors.

"Lo! in that house of misery
A lady with a lamp I see
  Pass through the glimmering gloom,
  And flit from room to room.

"And slow, as in a dream of bliss,
The speechless sufferer turns to kiss
  Her shadow, as it falls
  Upon the darkening walls."

"Ah," said to me old John Ball, the veteran of the Crimea, who had been wounded at Alma and been at Scutari a month before her arrival, so that in his later days there he saw the changes that she wrought, "ah, she was a *good* soul— she was a *good* woman!" And through his words, and those of the other old men who remembered her, it was possible to discern a little of the glow, the humour, the homely maternal tenderness with which the *Wohlgebohrene Dame* had comforted young and old in their hours of patriotic wounding and pain.

For herself, in the long days of sacrificial service,

was there any human solace, any dear companionship, any dawning light of love ?

For us at least, the mere outsiders, to whom
she is just a very practical saint and a very great
woman, " there lives no record of reply." But
we know that, though hers was the solitary path,
which yet was no solitude because of the out-
poured love and sympathy to others, when in
her presence once some one was chattering about
the advantages of " single blessedness," she, with
her quick sense of humour, replied that a fish
out of water might be blessed, but a good deal
of effort was needed to become accustomed to
the air !

None of the letters describing the Scutari life
are more interesting than those of Sister Aloysius,
the Irish Sister of Mercy, from whose graphic
descriptions quotations have already been made.

" She and her companions had had only a few
hours in which to prepare for a long and dangerous journey, with the details of which they were
quite unacquainted, only knowing that they were
to start for Turkey at half-past seven in the

morning, and that they went for the love of God.

" ' And who is to take care of you from this to Turkey ?' asked one of their amazed well-wishers. To which the Sisters only replied that ' they hoped their guardian angels would kindly do so.' "

Needless to say, the little party *did* reach its destination safely, and " at last," writes Sister Aloysius, " a despatch came * to say that five Sisters were to proceed to Scutari, to the General Hospital ; while arrangements were made for the other ten Sisters to proceed to a house on the Bosphorus, to await further orders. At once the five Sisters started for Scutari : Reverend Mother, Sister M. Agnes, Sister M. Elizabeth, Sister M. Winifred, and myself. When we reached Scutari we were shown to our quarters consisting of one little room, not in a very agreeable locality. However, we were quite satisfied none better could be found, and for this little nook we were thankful.

" Of course, we expected to be sent to the wards at once. Sister M. Agnes and the writer

* " Memories of the Crimea," by Sister Mary Aloysius. (Burns and Oates.)

were sent to a store to sort clothes that had been
eaten by the rats; Rev. Mother and Sister M.
Elizabeth either to the kitchen or to another
store. In a dark, damp, gloomy shed we set to
work and did the best we could; but, indeed,
the destruction accomplished by the rats was
something wonderful. On the woollen goods
they had feasted sumptuously. They were running about us in all directions; we begged of
the sergeant to leave the door open that we
might make our escape if they attacked us. Our
home rats would run if you 'hushed' them; but
you might 'hush' away, and the Scutari rats
would not take the least notice.

"During my stay in the stores I saw number-
less funerals pass by the window. Cholera was
raging, and how I did wish to be in the wards
amongst the poor dying soldiers! Before I leave
the stores I must mention that Sister M. Agnes
and myself thought the English nobility must
have emptied their wardrobes and linen stores to
send out bandages for the wounded—the most
beautiful underclothing, the finest cambric sheets,
with merely a scissors run here and there through

them to ensure their being used for no other purpose. And such large bales, too; some from the Queen's Palace, with the Royal monogram beautifully worked. Whoever sent out these immense bales thought nothing too good for the poor soldiers. And they were right—nothing was too good for them. And now good-bye stores and good-bye rats; for I was to be in the cholera wards in the morning.

"Where shall I begin, or how can I ever describe my first day in the hospital at Scutari? Vessels were arriving, and the orderlies carrying the poor fellows, who, with their wounds and frost-bites, had been tossing about on the Black Sea for two or three days, and sometimes more. Where were they to go? Not an available bed. They were laid on the floor one after another, till the beds were emptied of those dying of cholera and every other disease. Many died immediately after being brought in—their moans would pierce the heart—the taking of them in and out of the vessels must have increased their pain.

"The look of agony in those poor dying faces will never leave my heart.

"Week in, week out, the cholera went on. The same remedies were continued, though almost always to fail. However, while there was life there was hope, and we kept on the warm applications to the last. When it came near the end the patients got into a sort of collapse, out of which they did not rally.

"We begged the orderlies, waiting to take them to the dead-house, to wait a little lest they might not be dead; and with great difficulty we prevailed on them to make the least delay. As a rule the orderlies drank freely—'to drown their grief,' they said. I must say that their position was a very hard one—their work always increasing—and such work; death around them on every side; their own lives in continual danger —it was almost for them a continuation of the field of battle.

"The poor wounded men brought in out of the vessels were in a dreadful state of dirt, and so weak that whatever cleaning they got had to be done cautiously. Oh, the state of those fine fellows, so worn out with fatigue, so full of vermin! Most, or all, of them required spoon-feeding. We had wine, sago, arrowroot. Indeed, I think there was everything in the stores, but it was so hard to get them. . . . An orderly officer took the rounds of the wards every night to see that all was right. He was expected by the orderlies, and the moment he raised the latch one cried out, 'All right, your honour.' Many a time I said, 'All wrong.' The poor officer, of course, went his way; and one could scarcely blame him for not entering those wards, so filled with pestilence, the air so dreadful that to breathe it might cost him his life. And then, what could he do even if he did come? I remember one day an officer's orderly being brought in—a dreadful case of cholera; and so devoted was his master that he came in every half-hour to see him, and stood over him in the bed as if it was only a cold he had; the poor fellow died after a few hours' illness. I hope his devoted master escaped. I never heard.

"Each Sister had charge of two wards, and there was just at this time a fresh outbreak of cholera. The Sisters were up every night; and the cases, as in Scutari and Kullali, were nearly all fatal. Reverend Mother did not allow the Sisters to remain up all night, except in cases of cholera, without a written order from the doctor.

"In passing to the wards at night we used to meet the rats in droves. They would not even move out of our way. They were there before us, and were determined to keep possession. As for our hut, they evidently wanted to make it theirs, scraping under the boards, jumping up on the shelf where our little tin utensils were kept, rattling everything. One night dear Sister M. Paula found one licking her forehead—she had a real horror of them. Sleep was out of the question. Our third day in Balaclava was a very sad one for us. One of our dear band, Sister Winifred, got very ill during the night with cholera. She was a most angelic Sister, and we were all deeply grieved.

"She, the first to go of all our little band, had been full of life and energy the day before. We were all very sad, and we wondered who would be the next.

"Miss Nightingale was at the funeral, and

even joined in the prayers. The soldiers, doctors, officers, and officials followed. When all was over we returned to our hut, very sad; but we had no further time to think. Patients were pouring in, and we should be out again to the cholera wards. Besides cholera there were cases of fever—in fact, of every disease. Others had been nearly killed by the blasting of rocks, and they came in fearfully disfigured.

"Father Woolett brought us one day a present of a Russian cat; he bought it, he told us, from an old Russian woman for the small sum of seven shillings. It made a particularly handsome captive in the land of its fathers, for we were obliged to keep it tied to a chair to prevent its escape. But the very sight of this powerful champion soon relieved us of some of our unwelcome and voracious visitors.

"Early in 1856 rumours of peace reached us from all sides. But our Heavenly Father demanded another sacrifice from our devoted little band. Dear Sister Mary Elizabeth was called to a martyr's crown.

"She was specially beloved for her extraordinary sweetness of disposition. The doctor, when called, pronounced her illness to be fever; she had caught typhus in her ward. Every loving care was bestowed on her by our dearest Mother, who scarcely ever left her bedside. Death seemed to have no sting. . . . She had no wish to live or die, feeling she was in the arms of her Heavenly Father. 'He will do for me what is best,' she whispered, 'and His will is all I desire.'"

At Scutari Miss Nightingale's work of re-organization was bearing swift fruit. The wives of the soldiers were daily employed in the laundry she had established, so that they had a decent livelihood, and the soldiers themselves had clean linen. But, of course, a great many of the soldiers had left their wives and children at home.

A money office also had been formed by the Lady-in-Chief, which helped them in sending home their pay. It was she too who arranged for the safe return of the widows to England, and it was she who provided stamps and stationery for the men, that they might be able to write to those dear to them. No one had had a moment, it seemed, to give thought to anything but the actual warfare with all its horrors, until her womanly sympathy and splendid capacity came on the scene. With her there was always little time lost between planning and achieving, and happily she had power of every kind in her hand. Besides her own means, which she poured forth like water, the people of England had, as we saw, subscribed magnificently through the *Times* Fund, and with one so practical as the Lady-in-Chief in daily consultation with Mr. Macdonald, there was no longer any fear of giving to church walls what was intended to save the lives of ill-clad and dying soldiers.

CHAPTER XVII.

Miss Nightingale visits Balaclava—Her illness—Lord Raglan's visit—The Fall of Sebastopol.

AT last, in the May of 1855, the Lady-in-Chief was able to see such fruits of the six months' steady work at Scutari that the scene of her labours could be changed, and she set out for Balaclava to inspect the other hospitals, for which, as superintendent of the ladies in the military hospitals in the East, she was responsible. She wished to see for herself what was being done for the soldiers on the field. Besides Mr. Bracebridge and her nursing staff, M. Soyer accompanied her with a view to improving the cooking arrangements for the army in the field, and he writes with his usual vividness :—

" Thomas, Miss Nightingale's boy, the twelve-year-old drummer who had left what he called his 'instrument sticks' to make himself her most devoted slave and messenger, was also allowed to go.

"At nine," says M. Soyer, "we were all on shore and mounted. There were about eight of us ready to escort our heroine to the seat of war. Miss Nightingale was attired simply in a genteel amazone, or riding habit, and had quite a martial air. She was mounted upon a very pretty mare of a golden colour which, by its gambols and caracoling, seemed proud to carry its noble charge. The weather was very fine. Our cavalcade produced an extraordinary effect upon the motley crowd of all nations assembled at Balaclava, who were astonished at seeing a lady so well escorted. It was not so, however, with those who knew who the lady was."

Later he gives us a most characteristic glimpse of the light-hearted courage and high spirit of his Lady-in-Chief :—

"Mr. Anderson proposed to have a peep at Sebastopol. It was four o'clock, and they were firing sharply on both sides. Miss Nightingale,

to whom the offer was made, immediately accepted it; so we formed a column and,
for the first time, fearlessly faced the enemy,
and prepared to go under fire. P. M. turned
round to me, saying quietly, but with great
trepidation, 'I say, Monsieur Soyer, of course
you would not take Miss Nightingale where
there will be any danger?' . . . The sentry then
repeated his caution, saying, 'Madam, even
where you stand you are in great danger; some
of the shot reach more than half a mile beyond
this!' . . . 'My good young man,' replied Miss
Nightingale in French, 'more dead and wounded
have passed through my hands than I hope you
will ever see in the battlefield during the whole
of your military career; believe me, I have no
fear of death!'"

By a little guile the eager Frenchman led the
unsuspecting idol of the troops into a position
where she could be well seen by the soldiers;
and while she was seated on the Morta, in view
of them all, it hardly needed his own dramatic
outcry for a salutation to "the Daughter of Eng-

land" to call forth the ringing cheers which greeted her from the men of the 39th Regiment, and the shouts were taken up so loudly by all the rest that the Russians were actually startled by them at Sebastopol.

The darkness fell quickly, and half-way back to Balaclava Miss Nightingale and her party found themselves in the midst of a merry Zouave camp, where the men were singing and drinking coffee, but warned our friends that brigands were in the neighbourhood. However, there was nothing for it but to push on, and, as a matter of fact, the only wound received was from the head of Miss Nightingale's horse, which hit violently against the face of her escort at the bridle rein, who kept silence that he might not alarm her, but was found with a face black and bleeding at the end of the journey.

After her night's rest in her state-cabin in the *Robert Lowe*, though still feeling used up with the adventurous visit to the camp hospitals, Miss Nightingale visited the General Hospital at Balaclava and the collection of huts on the heights, which formed the sanatoria, and also went to see an officer ill with typhus in the doctors' huts. She renewed her visit next day, when, after a night at Balaclava, she settled three nurses into the sanatorium, and then for some days continued her inspection of hospitals and moved into the ship *London*, the *Robert Lowe* having been ordered home.

Worn out by her ceaseless labours at Scutari, she had probably been specially open to infection in the sick officer's hut, and while on board the *London* it became clear that she had contracted Crimean fever in a very bad form.

She was ordered up to the huts amid such dreadful lamentations of the surrounding folk that, thanks to their well-meant delays, it took an hour to carry her up to the heights, her faithful nurse, Mrs. Roberts, keeping off the sun-glare by walking beside her with an umbrella, and her page-boy Thomas weeping his heart out at the tail of the little procession.

A spot was found after her own heart near a running stream where the wild flowers were in bloom, and she tells in her *Nursing Notes* how her first recovery began when a nosegay of her beloved flowers was brought to her bedside. But for some days she was desperately ill, and the camp was unspeakably moved and alarmed.

Britain also shared deeply in the suspense, though happily the worst crisis was passed in about twelve days, leaving, however, a long time of great weakness and slow convalescence to be won through afterwards.

During those twelve days some very sharp skirmishing took place, and there was talk of an attack on Balaclava from the Kamara side, in which case Miss Nightingale's hut would, it was said, be the first outpost to be attacked. Any such notion was, of course, an injustice to the Russians, who would not knowingly have hurt a hair of her head—indeed, it may almost be said that she was sacred to all the troops, whether friends or foes. But at all events it gave her boy Thomas his opportunity, and he was prepared, we are told, "to die valiantly in defence of his mistress."

Soyer gives a picturesque account of Lord Raglan's visit to Miss Nightingale when her recovery was first beginning. He begins by describing his own visit, and tells the story through the lips of Mrs. Roberts, Miss Nightingale's faithful nurse.

" . . . I was," he writes, "very anxious to know the actual state of Miss Nightingale's health, and went to her hut to inquire. I found Mrs. Roberts, who was quite astonished and very much delighted to see me.

"'Thank God, Monsieur Soyer,' she exclaimed, 'you are here again. We have all been in such a way about you. Why, it was reported that you had been taken prisoner by the Russians. I must go and tell Miss Nightingale you are found again.'

"'Don't disturb her now. I understand Lord Raglan has been to see her.'

"'Yes, he has, and I made a serious mistake. It was about five o'clock in the afternoon when he came. Miss Nightingale was dozing, after a very restless night. We had a storm that day and it was very wet. I was in my room sewing when two men on horseback, wrapped in large gutta-percha cloaks and dripping wet, knocked at the door. I went out, and one inquired in which hut Miss Nightingale resided.

" ' He spoke so loud that I said, " Hist ! hist ! don't make such a horrible noise as that, my man," at the same time making a sign with both hands for him to be quiet. He then repeated his question, but not in so loud a tone. I told him this was the hut.

" ' " All right," said he, jumping from his horse, and he was walking straight in when I pushed him back, asking what he meant and whom he wanted.

" ' " Miss Nightingale," said he.

" ' " And pray who are you ? "

" ' " Oh, only a soldier," was the reply ; " but I must see her—I have come a long way—my name is Raglan : she knows me very well."

" ' Miss Nightingale, overhearing him, called me in, saying, " Oh ! Mrs. Roberts, it is Lord Raglan. Pray tell him I have a very bad fever, and it will be dangerous for him to come near me."

" ' " I have no fear of fever, or anything else," said Lord Raglan.

" ' And before I had time to turn round, in came his lordship. He took up a stool, sat down at the foot of the bed, and kindly asked Miss Nightingale how she was, expressing his sorrow at her illness, and thanking her and praising her for the good she had done for the troops. He wished her a speedy recovery, and hoped that she might be able to continue her charitable and invaluable exertions, so highly appreciated by every one, as well as by himself.

"'He then bade Miss Nightingale good-bye, and went away. As he was going I said I wished to apologize.

"'" No, no! not at all, my dear lady," said Lord Raglan ; " you did very right ; for I perceive that Miss Nightingale has not yet received my letter, in which I announced my intention of paying her a visit to-day—having previously inquired of the doctor if she could be seen." ' " *

The doctors, after her twelve days of dangerous illness, were urgent for Miss Nightingale's instant return to England ; but this she would not do : she was sure that, with time and patience, she would be able once more to take up her

* "Soyer's Culinary Campaign," Alexis Soyer. (Routledge, 1857.)

work at Scutari. Lord Ward placed his yacht at her disposal, and by slow degrees she made recovery, though Lord Raglan's death, June 18, 1855, was a great grief and shock to her.

Wellington said of Lord Raglan that he was a man who would not tell a lie to save his life, and he was also a man of great charm and benevolence, adored by his troops. He felt to the quick the terrible repulse of our troops before Sebastopol that June, having yielded his own counsels to those of France rather than break the alliance, and he died two days after the despatch was written in which he told the story of this event.

Writing to the Duke of Newcastle in October, he had entreated for his army a little repose— that brave army, worn out, not only by the ordinary fatigues of a military campaign, and by the actual collecting of wood and water to keep life from extinction, but by cholera, sickness, and the bitter purgatorial cold of a black hillside in a Russian winter.

"Repose!" echoes Kinglake with sardonic bitterness, and we too echo it, remembering how, two days afterwards, it was riding through the devil's jaws at Balaclava, to hurl itself but a little later against its myriad assailants at Inkermann !

Repose ! uncomplaining and loyal, in the bitter grasp of winter on the heights of the Chersonese, holding day and night a siege that seemed endless, the allied armies had proved their heroism through the slow tragedy.   And when at last, on the day of victory, amid the fury of the elements and the avenging fury of their own surging hearts, they grasped the result of their patient agony, though

> ' Stormed at with shot and shell,
> Boldly they rode and well,"

that final moment of onset did but crown the fortitude of those long, slow days of dying by inches in the slow clutch of starvation, that had been so much harder to bear, while they saw their comrades in the anguish of cholera and felt their own limbs freezing beneath them.

But it was doubtless a brave assault, and it was sad that their loved commander was not there to see ; for, while the Malakoff fell before the

French, it was the British troops that took the
Redan—that Redan of which it has been written
that "three months before it had repulsed the
attacking force with fearful carnage, and brought
Lord Raglan to a despairing death."

There is tragedy, therefore, in the fact that
when, so soon afterwards, Sebastopol fell, the
triumph was not his.

It was on September 8, amid a furious storm
which suddenly broke up a summer-like day,
that the cannonade joined with the thunder and
the final assault was made. Though the first
shouts of victory came at the end of an hour,
it was nightfall before the fighting ceased and
the Russians retreated. Sebastopol was in flames.
And before the next day dawned the last act in
this terrible war-drama was over.

Within a month of leaving Scutari Miss
Nightingale was already there again, and during
these days of slowly returning strength, when
she wandered sometimes through the beautiful
cemetery where the strange, black-plumaged
birds fly above the cypresses and, against the
background of the blue Bosphorus, the roses

garland the tombs, she planned, for the soldiers who had fallen, the monument which now stands there to their undying memory, where under the drooping wings of the angels that support it are inserted the words, " This monument was erected by Queen Victoria and her people."

CHAPTER XVIII.

The Nightingale Fund—Miss Nightingale remains at her post, organizing healthy occupations for the men off duty—Sisters of Mercy—The Queen's jewel—Its meaning.

FAR and wide spread the news of the fall of Sebastopol, and London took the lead in rejoicings. The Tower guns shouted the victory, the arsenals fired their salutes, cathedrals and village churches rang out their welcome to peace. There were sons, husbands, brothers, fathers, for whom there would be no more home-coming on earth; and some who would come back broken and maimed : but all had served their country, and heroism lasts beyond time and death.

All through the empire arose an outcry of thanksgiving to the woman who still remained at her post among the sick and the dying—the woman who had saved England's honour in the day of disgrace and neglect, and had saved also countless lives among her brave sons.

The Queen and all her people were eager to know what there was that they might lay at her feet. In one form only would Miss Nightingale accept the testimony offered—namely, the means of yet further work. The Herberts knew she had longed to organize a hospital on the lines of unpaid nursing, but there was a difficulty for the moment, because she could not bring herself to leave the East until her work there was fully completed, and such a hospital must, they thought, have her presence from the first. Just now she was with Sister Aloysius at Balaclava, nursing one of her staff, and while there an accident on the rough roads, which injured not only herself, but also the Sister who was walking beside her, led to a thoughtful kindness from Colonel Macmurdo, who had a little carriage especially made for her. In this little carriage, through the cutting cold and snow of a Crimean winter, she would drive about among the camp hospitals with no escort but her driver, as she returned through the dark night at the end of her

long day of self-imposed duties. Sometimes she
has stood for hours on a cold, shelterless rock,
giving her directions, and when one and another
of her friends entreated against such risk and
exposure, she would just smile with a quiet
certainty that, for all that in her eyes was her
clear duty, strength and protection would .
certainly be given.

She was much occupied in helping and
uplifting the convalescent, and not only these,
but also all the soldiers in camp in the army
of occupation, which was for a while to be left
in the East until the treaty was signed, and would
necessarily be surrounded by special temptations
in time of peace. Her way of fighting drunkenness—and after Sebastopol you may be sure there
was a good deal of " drinking of healths "—was
to provide all possible means of interest and
amusement. Huts were built, clubs were formed.
Stationery was provided for letters home. So
effectually was every one in England interested
that, while Queen Victoria herself led the way in
sending newspapers and magazines, all through
the country her example was followed.

And while this was going on, the great testimonial fund in London was mounting and mounting.

The Duke of Cambridge, Lord Houghton, and the Marquis of Ripon were members of the committee. The great bankers opened their books. The churches collected funds, *the rank and file of our impoverished army sent* £4,000, and taking Mrs. Tooley's figures, which are doubtless correct, and including all ranks and all troops throughout the world, the military contributions alone appear to have risen to about £10,000.

Jenny Lind, then Madame Goldschmidt, gave a concert, of which she herself bore all the expense, amounting to about £500, and then gave the entire proceeds, about £2,000, to the fund. This was so warmly appreciated by some of those interested in the success of the fund that, by private subscription, they gave a marble bust of Queen Victoria to the Goldschmidts as a thank-offering.

From the overseas dominions came over £4,000 ; from provincial cities, towns, and villages in Britain, between £6,000 and £7,000, and from British residents abroad also a very handsome sum. Indeed, it may be truly said that in every quarter of the globe men and women united to pour forth their gratitude to Miss Nightingale, and to enable her to complete the work so bravely begun, by transforming the old and evil methods of nursing under British rule to that ideal art in which fortitude, tenderness, and skill receive their crowning grace. It has been said—I know not with what exactitude—that no British subject has ever received such world-wide honour as was at this time laid at her feet.

At one of the great meetings Mr. Sidney Herbert read the following letter from one of his friends :—

"I have just heard a pretty account from a soldier describing the comfort it was even to see Florence pass. 'She would speak to one and another,' he said, 'and nod and smile to many more, but she could not do it to all, you know, for we lay there by hundreds ; but we could kiss

her shadow * as it fell, and lay our heads on
the pillow again content.' "

That letter alone, we are told, brought another
£10,000.

The gross amount had reached £44,000,
but in 1857 Miss Nightingale desired that
the list should be closed and help be given
instead to our French Allies, who were then
suffering from the terrible floods that laid waste
their country in that year.

And whatever she commanded, of course, was
done.   Alike in England and in the Crimea, her
influence was potent for all good.

She herself was still busy nursing some of the
Roman Catholic members of her staff in the huts
on the snowclad heights of Balaclava, and how
heartily she valued them may be judged from
these closing sentences of a letter to their
Reverend Mother :—

" You know that I shall do everything I can

---

* I know not whether this was the man whose arm she had
saved ; probably many others echoed his feeling, and he was not
by any means the only soldier who thus reverently greeted her
passing presence.

for the Sisters whom you have left me. I will care for them as if they were my own children. But it will not be like you."

Not very far from the sanatorium on the heights above Balaclava, two new camp hospitals had been put up, and while superintending the nursing there, our Lady-in-Chief lived in a three-roomed hut with a medical store attached to it, where she was quite near to sanatorium and hospitals. She and the three Sisters who were with her had not very weather-proof quarters. One of them, whose letters are full of interest, tells of their waking one morning to find themselves covered with snow, and leading a life of such adventurous simplicity that when the Protestant chaplain brought some eggs tied up in a handkerchief the gift was regarded as princely ! Happily, they were able to reward the gentleman by washing his neckties, and ironing them with an ingenious makeshift for the missing flat-iron, in the shape of a teapot filled with hot water. Every night everything in the huts froze, even to the ink. But Miss Nightingale tells how brave

Miss Nightingale's Medals and Decorations.

and entirely self-forgetful the Sisters were under every hardship and privation.

By those who have never had the privilege of knowing such women intimately, her affection for them may be the better understood from the following graphic letter written by Lord Napier :—

"At an early period of my life I held a diplomatic position under Lord Stratford de Redcliffe in Constantinople. During the distress of the Crimean War the Ambassador called me one morning and said : ' Go down to the port ; you will find a ship there loaded with Jewish exiles—Russian subjects from the Crimea. It is your duty to disembark them. The Turks will give you a house in which they may be placed. I turn them over entirely to you.' I went down to the shore and received about two hundred persons, the most miserable objects that could be witnessed, most of them old men, women, and children. I placed them in the cold, ruinous lodging allocated to them by the Ottoman authorities. I went back to the Ambassador and said : ' Your Excellency, these people are cold, and I have no fuel or blankets. They are hungry, and I have no food. They are dirty, and I have no soap. Their hair is in an indescribable condition, and I have no combs. What am I to do with these people ? ' ' Do ? ' said the Ambassador. ' Get a couple of Sisters of Mercy ; they will put all to right in a moment.' I went, saw the Mother Superior, and explained the case. I asked for two Sisters. She ordered two from her presence to follow me. They were ladies of refinement and intellect. I was a stranger and a Protestant, and I invoked their assistance for the benefit of the Jews. Yet these two women made up their bundles and followed me through the rain, without a look, a whisper, a sign of hesitation. From that moment my fugitives were saved. I witnessed the labours of those Sisters for months, and they never endeavoured to make a single convert."

The military men were not less enthusiastic. When Colonel Connolly, brother-in-law to Mr. Bruin, of Carlow, was travelling,

after his return from the war, near the Bruin
estate, a fellow-traveller spoke disrespectfully
of nuns. The colonel, a Protestant, not only
made a warm defence of the ladies who had
nursed him in Russia and Ottoman regions, and
for their sakes of all other nuns, but handed the
assailant his card, saying : " If you say another
word against these saintly gentlewomen I shall
call you out." The slanderer subsided very
quickly.

Sister Aloysius, one of those very Sisters who
were with Miss Nightingale in the huts, has
written in her " Memories of the Crimea " :—

" It was said at one time that the War Office
was on the point of issuing a mandate forbidding
us to speak even to the Catholic soldiers on
religion, or to say a prayer for them. However,
that mandate never came ; we often thought the
guardian angels of the soldiers prevented it."

It made no difference to the loyalty of their
work together that Miss Nightingale was not a
Roman Catholic ; they all obeyed the Master who
has taught that it is not the way in which He is

addressed that matters, but whether we help those whom He gave His life to help, and in loving and serving whom, we love and serve Him.

So in London and in Balaclava the good of her influence was felt. In London the funds mounted, and at Balaclava the excellent work among the soldiers still went on.

Her very presence among the men helped to keep them sober and diligent, and in every way at their best, in those first months of victory when heads are only too easily turned. And she had the reward she most desired, for she was able to speak of these brave fellows—the nameless heroes of the long campaign—as having been "uniformly quiet and well-bred." Those words, it is true, were spoken of the men attending the reading-huts ; but they are quite in line with her more general verdict with regard to Tommy ; though, alas, we cannot stretch them to cover his behaviour at the canteens, where we are told that much drunkenness prevailed.

She had advanced money for the building of a coffee-house at Inkermann, and had helped the chaplain to get maps and slates for his school work, and the bundles of magazines and illustrated papers, sent out from England in answer to her appeal, as well as books sent out by the Duchess of Kent, cheered and brightened many a long hour for the men. She was always on the alert to help them about sending home their pay, and quick to care for the interests of their wives and children.

Before she left the Crimea, her hut was beset by fifty or sixty poor women who had been left behind when their husbands sailed for home with their regiments. They had followed their husbands to the war without leave and, having proved themselves useful, had been allowed to remain. And now they were left alone in a strange land and, but for Florence Nightingale, the end of the story might have been bitter sorrow. But she managed to get them sent home in a British ship.

Many a mother at home must already have blessed her ; for reckless boys who had enlisted, without the sanction of their families, had again and again been by her persuaded to write home, and in the first months of the war she had actually undertaken to stamp for the men any letters home which were sent to her camp. And at Scutari she had arranged a provisional money-order office where, four afternoons in each week, she received from the men the pay which she encouraged them to send home. When we are told that, in small sums, about £1,000 passed through this office month by month, we realize dimly something of the labour involved, and thinking of all her other cares and labours, which were nevertheless not allowed to stand in the way of such practical thoughtfulness as this, we do not wonder that "the services" loved her with a love that was akin to worship. The money, as she herself says, "was literally so much rescued from the canteens and from drunkenness;" and the Government, following her lead, had themselves established money-order offices later at Scutari, Balaclava, Constantinople, and the Headquarters, Crimea.

It is not surprising that, in the "Old Country," songs were dedicated to her as "the good angel of Derbyshire," and that her very portrait became a popular advertisement.

And we have it on good authority that her name was revered alike by English, French, Turks, and Russians.

The Treaty of Peace was signed at Paris on March 30, 1856, and on July 12 General Codrington formally gave up Sebastopol and Balaclava to the Russians. When the last remnant of our army was ordered home and the hospitals were finally closed, Florence Nightingale was for the first time willing to leave a post which she had held so bravely and so long. But before she left she wished to leave a memorial to the brave men who had fallen, and the brave women, her comrades, who had died upon that other battlefield where disease, and Death himself, must be wrestled with on behalf of those who are nursed and tended.

And so it comes to pass that among the visible tokens which the war has left behind, is a gigantic white marble cross erected by Florence Nightingale upon the sombre heights of Balaclava, where it still opens wide its arms for every gleam of golden sunlight, every reflected shimmer, through the dark night, of silvery moon

and star, to hearten the sailors voyaging north-
ward and mark a prayer for the brave men and
women who toiled and suffered there. It is
inscribed with the words in Italian, " Lord, have
mercy upon us." But while she herself asked
only mercy for herself and others, that human
shortcomings might be forgiven, her compatriots
were uniting to do her honour.

On December 20, 1855, the *Morning Post*
printed the following announcement :—

" The country will experience much satisfaction, though no surprise, on learning, as we
believe we are correct in stating, that Her
Majesty the Queen has, in a manner as honourable to herself as it must be gratifying to her
people, been pleased to mark her warm appreciation of the unparalleled self-devotion of the good
Miss Nightingale. The Queen has transmitted
to that lady a jewelled ornament of great beauty,
which may be worn as a decoration, and has
accompanied it with an autograph letter—such
a letter as Queen Victoria has ere now proved
she can write—a letter not merely of graceful

acknowledgment, but full of that deep feeling which speaks from heart to heart, and at once ennobles the sovereign and the subject."

Of the symbolic meaning of this jewel the following exposition appeared in the issue of January 15, 1856, of the same paper :—

" The design of the jewel is admirable, and the effect no less brilliant than chaste.   It is characteristic and emblematical—being formed of a St. George's cross in ruby-red enamel, on a white field — representing England.   This is encircled by a black band, typifying the office of Charity, on which is inscribed a golden legend, ' Blessed are the merciful.'   The Royal donor is expressed by the letters ' V. R.' surmounted by a crown in diamonds, impressed upon the centre of the St. George's cross, from which also rays of gold emanating upon the field of white enamel are supposed to represent the glory of England. While spreading branches of palm, in bright green enamel, tipped with gold, form a framework for the shield, their stems at the bottom being banded with a ribbon of blue enamel (the colour of the ribbon for the Crimean medal), on which, in golden letters, is inscribed ' Crimea.' At the top of the shield, between the palm branches, and connecting the whole, three brilliant stars of diamonds illustrate the idea of the light of heaven shed upon the labours of Mercy, Peace, and Charity, in connection with the glory of a nation. On the back of this Royal jewel is an inscription on a golden tablet, written by Her Majesty . . . recording it to be a gift and testimonial in memory of services rendered to her brave army by Miss Nightingale. The jewel is about three inches in depth by two and a half in width. It is to be worn, not as a brooch or ornament, but rather as the badge of an order. We believe the credit of the design is due to the illustrious consort of Her Majesty."

Punch, of course, had always taken the liveliest interest in Miss Nightingale's work, and having begun with friendly jesting, he ended with a tribute so tender in its grave beauty that it would hardly have been out of place in a

church window ; for below a sketch of Florence
Nightingale herself, holding a wounded soldier
by the hand, and with the badge of Scutari
across her breast, was a vision of the Good
Samaritan.

CHAPTER XIX.

*Her citizenship—Her initiative—Public recognition and gratitude—
Her return incognito—Village excitement—The country's welcome—Miss Nightingale's broken health—The Nightingale
Fund—St. Thomas's Hospital—Reform of nursing as a
profession.*

IT may be fairly supposed that even those
benighted Philistines whose mockery had at the
outset been of a less innocent quality than
Punch's gentle fun, now found it expedient to
alter their tone, and if their objections had been
mere honest stupidity, they were probably both
convinced of their past folly and a good deal
ashamed.

For Britain was very proud of the daughter
who had become so mighty a power for good in
the State. The Sister of Mercy whom Miss
Nightingale used laughingly to call "her Cardinal"
had responded on one occasion by addressing her
with equal affection as " Your Holiness," and the

nickname was not altogether inappropriate, for
her advice in civic and hygienic matters had an
authority which might well be compared with
that which the Pope himself wielded on theo-
logical questions.

Among the doctors at Scutari was a friend of
General Evatt, from whom he had many facts at
first-hand, and it was therefore not without
knowledge that, in his conversation with me on
the subject, the latter confirmed and strengthened
all that has already been written of Miss Nightingale's mental grasp and supreme capacity. To
him, knowing her well, and knowing well also
the facts, she was the highest embodiment of
womanhood and of citizenship. Yet, while he
talked, my heart ached for her, thinking of the
womanly joys of home and motherhood which
were not for her, and all the pure and tender
romance which woman bears in her inmost
soul, even when, as in this noble instance, it is
transmuted by the will of God and the woman's
own obedient will into service of other homes
and other lives.

Perhaps I may here be allowed to quote a

sentence from Mrs. Tooley's admirable life of our heroine ; for it could not have been better expressed : " No one would wish to exempt from due praise even the humblest of that 'Angel Band' who worked with Florence Nightingale, and still less would she, but in every great cause there is the initiating genius who stands in solitary grandeur above the rank and file of followers."

Nor was official recognition of the country's debt to Miss Nightingale in any wise lacking. When the Treaty of Peace was under discussion in the House of Lords, Lord Ellesmere made it an opportunity for the following tribute :—

" My Lords, the agony of that time has become a matter of history. The vegetation of two successive springs has obscured the vestiges of Balaclava and of Inkermann. Strong voices now answer to the roll-call, and sturdy forms now cluster round the colours. The ranks are full, the hospitals are empty. The Angel of Mercy still lingers to the last on the scene of her labours ; but her mission is all but accomplished. Those long arcades of Scutari, in which dying men sat up to catch the sound of her footstep or the flutter of her dress, and fell back on the pillow content to have seen her shadow as it passed, are now comparatively deserted. She may probably be thinking how to escape, as best she may, on her return, the demonstrations of a nation's appreciation of the deeds and motives of Florence Nightingale."

And in the House of Commons Mr. Sidney Herbert said : " I have received, not only from medical men, but from many others who have had an opportunity of making observations, letters couched in the highest possible terms of praise. I will not repeat the words, but no higher expressions of praise could be applied to woman, for the wonderful energy, the wonderful tact, the wonderful tenderness, combined with the extraordinary self-devotion, which have been displayed by Miss Nightingale."

Lord Ellesmere was right when he hinted

that Miss Nightingale would be likely to do her best to escape all public fuss on her return. The Government had offered her a British man-of-war to take her home; but it was not her way to accept any such outward pomp, and, almost before people knew what had happened, it was found that she had travelled quietly home as Miss Smith in a French vessel, visiting in Paris her old friends the Sisters of St. Vincent de Paul, and finding that by having embarked at night, at a moment when Scutari was not looking for her departure, her little *ruse* had been very successful. An eager people had not recognized under the passing incognito of Miss Smith, travelling with her aunt, Mrs. Smith, the great Florence Nightingale whose return they had wished to celebrate. The village gossips at Lea Hurst have it that " the closely veiled lady in black, who slipped into her father's house by the back door, was first recognized by the family butler," and it seems a pity to spoil such a picturesque tradition by inquiring into it too closely.

There was great joy among the villagers that

The Nightingale Nursing Carriage.

"Miss Florence had come home from the wars," but it was understood that she wished to be quiet, and that bonfires and such-like rejoicings were out of the question.

Along the roads near Lea Hurst came troops of people from Derby and Nottingham, and even from Manchester, hoping to catch a glimpse of her; and there is in one of the biographies a vivid account, given by the old lady who kept the lodge gates, of how the park round Lea Hurst was beset by these lingering crowds, how men came without arms or without legs, hoping to see the Queen of Nurses. " But," added the old lady, " the squire wasn't a-going to let Miss Florence be made a staring-stock of." And, indeed, " Miss Florence " must have been in great need of repose, though never to the end of her life would it seem that she was allowed to have much of it ; for the very fruitfulness of her work made work multiply upon her hands, and her friend Mrs. Sidney Herbert knew her well when she said that to Florence Nightingale the dearest guerdon of work already done was the gift of more work still to do.

Perhaps we shall never any of us fully know what it must have been to one so abounding in spiritual energy and world-wide compassion to have to learn slowly and painfully, through the years that followed, what must henceforth be the physical limitations of her life. When we think of the long, careful training that had been given to her fine gifts of eye and hand in the art that she loved—for she rightly regarded nursing as an art—an art in which every movement must be a skilled and disciplined movement—we may divine something of what it cost to bear, without one murmur of complaint, what she might so easily have been tempted to regard as a lifelong waste of faculty. Instead of allowing herself to dwell on any such idea, gradually, as the knowledge dawned on her of what she must forego, she gave herself, with tenfold power in other directions, to work which *could* be achieved from an invalid's couch, and thus helped and guided others in that art all over the world.

Among the greetings which pleased her most on her first return to England was an address from the workmen of Newcastle-on-

Tyne, to whom she replied in the following
letter :—

August 23, 1856.

" My Dear Friends,—I wish it were in my
power to tell you what was in my heart when I
received your letter.

" Your welcome home, your sympathy with
what has been passing while I have been absent,
have touched me more than I can tell in words.
My dear friends, the things that are the deepest
in our hearts are perhaps what it is most difficult
for us to express. 'She hath done what she
could.' These words I inscribed on the tomb of
one of my best helpers when I left Scutari. It
has been my endeavour, in the sight of God, to do
as she has done.

" I will not speak of reward when permitted
to do our country's work—it is what we live
for—but I may say to receive sympathy from
affectionate hearts like yours is the greatest support, the greatest gratification, that it is possible
for me to receive from man.

" I thank you all, the eighteen hundred, with
grateful, tender affection. And I should have

written before to do so, were not the business,
which my return home has not ended, been
almost more than I can manage.—Pray believe
me, my dear friends, yours faithfully and
gratefully,   FLORENCE NIGHTINGALE."

Among the tokens of regard which the late
Duke of Devonshire brought to his old friend on
her return, when he drove over from Chatsworth
to Lea Hurst to see her after her long, eventful
absence, was a little silver owl, a sort of souvenir,
I suppose, of her beloved little "Athena," whose
death she had felt so keenly when leaving for the
Crimea.   Queen Victoria and the young princesses
were eager to welcome Miss Nightingale to Bal-
moral; and in looking back on her little visit
there, which seems to have been a happiness on
both sides, it is interesting to see how her
influence told upon the Crown Princess and   .
Princess Alice in their later organization of
hospital work, and to be reminded by Mrs.
Tooley, whose words we here venture to quote,
that the "tiny Princess Helena was to become
in after years an accomplished nurse, and an

active leader in the nursing movement of this
country; and, alas, to yield her soldier son on
the fatal field of South Africa."

Meanwhile, before and after this visit, Miss
Nightingale was quietly receiving her own friends
and neighbours at Lea Hurst, and entertaining
little parties of villagers from among the rustics
she had so long known and loved. Rich and
poor alike were all so eager to do her honour
that it is impossible to speak separately of all the
many forms which their expressions of gratitude
took. They included a gift from the workmen
of Sheffield as well as from her own more
immediate neighbours, and found their climax
in the fund pressed upon her by a grateful
nation, and for convenience called the Nightingale Fund, which was still awaiting its final
disposal.

Meanwhile, imagine the importance of the ex-
drummer-boy Thomas, her devoted servant and
would-be defender at Balaclava, promoted now
to be "Miss Nightingale's own man" in her
home at Lea Hurst—an even more exciting
presence to the villagers than the Russian hound

which was known through the country-side as
" Miss Florence's Crimean dog."

There were still living, we are told, when Mrs.
Tooley wrote her delightful record, a few old
people round about Lea Hurst who remembered
those great days of " Miss Florence's return,"
and the cannon balls and bullets they had seen as
trophies, the dried flowers gathered at Scutari,
and Thomas's thrilling stories, for if he had not
himself been present in the famous charge at
Balaclava, he did at least know all about it at
first-hand.

So little did any one dream that Miss Nightingale's health had been permanently shattered
that when the Indian Mutiny broke out in 1857,
she offered to go out to her friend Lady Canning,
and organize a nursing staff for the troops. And
while, with her customary business-like clearness,
she proceeded to draw up a detailed account of
all the private gifts entrusted to her for the
Crimea, and took the opportunity of putting on
record her tribute to Lord Raglan, the final
arrangements with regard to the Nightingale
Fund were still for a time held in suspense, in

the hope that she would so far recover strength
as to be able to take into her own hands the
government of that institution for the training of
hospital nurses, to which it was to be devoted.
When her friend Mr. Herbert talked gaily in
public of chaining her to the oar for the rest of
her life, that she might "raise the system of
nursing to a pitch of efficiency never before
known," he did not foresee that the invisible
chain, which was to bruise her eager spirit, was
to be of a kind so much harder to bear.   But
when, in 1860, her health showed no signs of
recovery, she definitely handed over to others
the management of the fund, only reserving to
herself the right to advise.   Her friend Mr.
Herbert was, up to the time of his death, the
guiding spirit of the council, and it gave Miss
Nightingale pleasure that St. Thomas's Hospital
should from the outset be associated with the
scheme, because that hospital had originated in
one of the oldest foundations in the country for
the relief of the sick poor, and in choosing it for
the training of lay sisters as nurses, its earliest
tradition was being continued.   The work of

the fund began at St. Thomas's in 1860, in the old building near London Bridge, before it moved into its present palace at Westminster, of which the Nightingale Training Home is a part. In those first early days an upper floor was arranged for the nurses in a new part of the old hospital, with a bedroom for each probationer, two rooms for the Sister-in-charge, and a sitting-room in which all shared. As the result of the advertisement for candidates in 1860, fifteen probationers were admitted in June, the first superintendent being Mrs. Wardroper. The probationers were, of course, under the authority of the matron, and subject to the rules of the hospital. They were to give help in the wards and receive teaching from the Sisters and medical staff, and if at the end of the year they passed their examination, they were to be registered as certified nurses.

Thanks to Miss Nightingale and other pioneers, the fifty years that have passed since then have made Mrs. Grundy a little less Grundyish, but in those days she considered the whole business a terrible venture, and was too much occupied

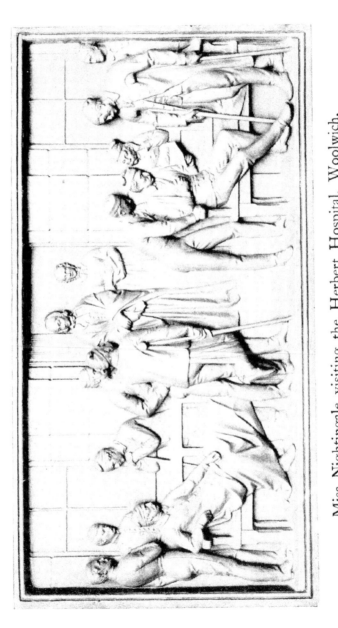

Miss Nightingale visiting the Herbert Hospital, Woolwich.

(Bas-relief on the pedestal—Herbert Memorial.)

with the idea of possible love affairs between the
doctors and nurses to realize what good work
was being done. The first year was a very
anxious one for Miss Nightingale, but all the
world knows now how her experiment has
justified itself and how her prayers have been
answered; for it was in prayer that she found
her "quietness and confidence" through those
first months of tension when the enemy was
watching and four probationers had to be dismissed, though their ranks were speedily filled
up by others.

At the end of the year, from among those who
were placed on the register, six received appoint-
ments at St. Thomas's and two took work in
infirmaries. There was special need of good
nurses in workhouse infirmaries, and there was
also throughout the whole country a crying need
for nurses carefully trained in midwifery : lack of
knowledge, for instance, had greatly increased
the danger of puerperal fever, a scourge against
which Miss Nightingale was one of the first
to contend ; and it had been wisely decided that
while two-thirds of the fund should go to the

work at St. Thomas's, one-third should be used for special training of nurses in these branches at King's College.

"How has the tone and state of hospital nurses been raised ? " Miss Nightingale asks in her little book on "Trained Nursing for the Sick Poor," published in 1876.

"By, more than anything else, making the hospital such a home as good young women—educated young women—can live and nurse in; and, secondly, by raising hospital nursing into such a profession as these can earn an honourable livelihood in."

In her "Notes on Hospitals," published in 1859, she pointed out what she considered the four radical defects in hospital construction—namely :—

1. The agglomeration of a large number of sick under the same roof.
2. Deficiency of space.
3. Deficiency of ventilation.
4. Deficiency of light.

How magnificently builders have since learned to remedy such defects may be seen in the Nightingale Wing of St. Thomas's Hospital.

The block system on which St. Thomas's Hospital is built is what Miss Nightingale has always recommended, each block being divided from the next by a space of 125 feet, across which runs a double corridor by means of which they communicate with one another. Each has three tiers of wards above the ground floor.

The six blocks in the centre are those used for patients, that at the south for the lecture-rooms and a school of medicine, the one at the north, adjoining Westminster Bridge, for the official staff. From Lambeth Palace to Westminster Bridge, with a frontage of 1,700 feet, the hospital extends; and there would be room in the operating theatre for 600 students. In the special wing in one of the northern blocks, reserved for the Nightingale Home and Training School for Nurses, everything has been ordered in accordance with Miss Nightingale's wishes.

To-day the whole *status* of nursing in Britain and British dominions is recognized as that of an

honoured and certified profession, and year by
year, at St. Thomas's alone, thirty probationers
are trained, of whom fifteen pay £1, 1s. a week
for the privilege, whereas to the other fifteen it
is given gratuitously.   At St. Thomas's were
trained nurses who were among the earliest to
be decorated with the Red Cross, that international badge of good army nursing throughout
the world which, indirectly as well as directly,
owed much to Miss Nightingale.   How warmly,
even arduously, Miss Nightingale shared in the
trials and joys and adventures of her nurses, comes
out very clearly in some of her letters to one of
them, whom, as a personal friend and one of the
first nine to receive the Red Cross, she playfully
named "her Cape of Good Hope."   Those tender
and intimate letters, which I will not name
emotional, because she who wrote them had
justified emotion by ever translating it into
useful work, made me feel to an almost startling
degree her warm, eager, dominating personality
with its extraordinary mingling of utmost modesty
and pleading authority.   To me that personality
seems to win the heart of the coldest and dullest

by its ardent enthusiasm and humility, and those unpublished letters, which I was privileged to read, brought home to me how Miss Nightingale —then an invalid of sixty-two—literally *lived* in the life of those pioneer nurses whom she had inspired and sent forth.

It is easy to see in them how much she feared for her nurses any innocent little trip of the tongue, with regard to the rest of the staff, which might set rolling the dangerous ball of hospital gossip. She puts the duty of obedience and forbearance on the highest grounds, and she draws a useful distinction between the sham dignity which we all know in the hatefulness of "the superior person," and the true dignity which tries to uplift those less fortunate, rather than self-indulgently to lean on them or make to them foolish confidences.

And while she is all aglow with sympathy for every detail of a nurse's work, she entreats her friend to "let no want of concord or discretion appear to mar that blessed work. And let no one," she adds, "be able justly to say what was said to me last month, ' It is only Roman Catholic vows that can keep Sisters together.' "

What she wrote when asking for recruits for St. Thomas's at the outset still remains the basis of the ideal held there. "We require," she wrote, "that a woman be sober, honest, truthful, without which there is no foundation on which to build.

"We train her in habits of punctuality, quietness, trustworthiness, personal neatness. We teach her how to manage the concerns of a large ward or establishment. We train her in dressing wounds and other injuries, and in performing all those minor operations which nurses are called upon day and night to undertake.

"We teach her how to manage helpless patients in regard to moving, changing, feeding, temperature, and the prevention of bedsores.

"She has to make and apply bandages, line splints, and the like. She must know how to make beds with as little disturbance as possible to their inmates. She is instructed how to wait at operations, and as to the kind of aid the surgeon requires at her hands. She is taught cooking for the sick; the principle on which sick wards ought to be cleansed, aired, and warmed ; the management of convalescents ; and how to observe sick and maimed patients, so as to give an intelligent and truthful account to the physician or surgeon in regard to the progress of cases in the intervals between visits—a much more difficult thing than is generally supposed.

"We do not seek to make 'medical women,' but simply nurses acquainted with the principle which they are required constantly to apply at the bedside.

"For the future superintendent is added a course of instruction in the administration of a hospital, including, of course, the linen arrangements, and what else is necessary for a matron to be conversant with.

"There are those who think that all this is intuitive in women, that they are born so, or, at least, that it comes to them without training. To such we say, by all means send us as many such geniuses as you can, for we are sorely in want of them."

CHAPTER XX.

A word must here be said of Mr. William Rathbone's work in Liverpool. After the death of his first wife, realizing the comfort and help that had been given during her last illness by a trained nurse, he determined to do what he could to bring aid of the same kind into the homes of the poor, where the need was often so much more terrible. This brought him into touch with Miss Nightingale, who advised him to start a school of nursing in connection with the Liverpool Hospital. These two friends—for they soon became trusted and valued friends, each to each—were both people of prompt and efficient action, and one step led to another, until Liverpool had not only an important school of nurses for the sick poor, but also led the way throughout the country in the reform of the hitherto scandalous nursing in workhouse infirmaries. Mr. Rathbone set his mind on securing the services of Miss Agnes Elizabeth Jones to help him in his work, a woman of character as saintly as his own, and the difference in their religious outlook only made more beautiful their mutual relations in this great work.

Miss Agnes Jones, who has already been mentioned more than once in these pages, left an undying record on England's roll of honour. It was of her that in 1868 Miss Nightingale wrote *:—

" A woman attractive and rich, and young and witty ; yet a veiled and silent woman, distinguished by no other genius but the divine genius—working hard to train herself in order to train others to walk in the footsteps of Him who went about doing good. . . . She died, as she had lived, at her post in one of the largest workhouse infirmaries in this kingdom—the first in which trained nursing has been introduced. . . .

* "Introduction to Memorials of Agnes Elizabeth Jones." Reprinted from *Good Words* for June 1868. Florence Nightingale.

When her whole life and image rise before me, so far from thinking the story of Una and her lion a myth, I say here is Una in real flesh and blood—Una and her paupers far more untamable than lions. In less than three years she had reduced one of the most disorderly hospital populations in the world to something like Christian discipline, and had converted a vestry to the conviction of the economy as well as humanity of nursing pauper sick by trained nurses."

And it was in introducing a book about the Liverpool Home and School for Nurses that she wrote :—

"Nursing, especially that most important of all its branches—nursing of the sick poor at home —is no amateur work. To do it as it ought to be done requires knowledge, practice, self-abnegation, and, as is so well said here, direct obedience to and activity under the highest of all masters and from the highest of all motives. It is an essential part of the daily service of the Christian Church. It has never been otherwise. It has proved itself superior to all religious divi-

sions, and is destined, by God's blessing, to supply
an opening the great value of which, in our
densely populated towns, has been unaccountably
overlooked until within these few years."

As early as 1858 Miss Nightingale published
" Notes on Matters affecting the Health, Efficiency, and Hospital Administration of the
British Army," and the commission on this
subject appointed in 1857 set a high value on
her evidence.

Something of the development that followed
along both these lines—that of army reform and
of nursing among the submerged—may be
gleaned from the following clear statement of
fact which appeared during the South African
War, on May 21, 1900, in a great London
daily :—

" In the forty and more years that have elapsed
since her return, Miss Nightingale has seen the
whole system of army nursing and hospitals
transformed.   Netley, which has been visited
by the Queen again this week, was designed by
her, and for the next largest, namely, the Her-

bert Hospital, Woolwich, she assisted and advised
Sir Douglas Galton in his plans.

"There is not a naval or military hospital on
any of the foreign stations or depôts on which
she has not been consulted, and matters concerning the health and well-being of both services
have been constantly brought before her.   District nursing owes much to her, and in this
connection may be cited a few lines from a letter
which she wrote when Princess Louise, Duchess
of Argyll, was initiating a movement to establish
a home for the Queen's Jubilee Nurses in Chis-
wick and Hammersmith.   'I look upon district
nursing,' she wrote, 'as one of the most hopeful
of the agencies for raising the poor, physically
as well as morally, its province being not only
nursing the patient, but nursing the room, show-
ing the family and neighbours how to second the
nurse, and eminently how to nurse health as well
as disease.' "

"Everywhere," we read in Mr. Stephen Paget's
contribution to the "Dictionary of National Biography," "her expert reputation was paramount,"

and "during the American Civil War of 1862–4, and the Franco-German War of 1870–1, her advice was eagerly sought by the governments concerned." The "Dictionary of National Biography" also assures us that "in regard to civil hospitals, home nursing, care of poor women in childbirth, and sanitation, Miss Nightingale's authority stood equally high."

In what she wrote there was a homely directness, a complete absence of anything like pose or affectation, which more than doubled her power, and was the more charming in a woman of such brilliant acquirements and—to quote once more Dean Stanley's words — such " commanding genius " ; but, then, genius is of its nature opposed to all that is sentimental or artificial.

I believe it is in her " Notes on Nursing for the Labouring Classes " that she writes to those who are " minding baby " : " One-half of all the nurses in service are girls of from five to twenty years old. You see you are very important little people. Then there are all the girls who are nursing mother's baby at home ; and in all these cases it seems pretty nearly to come to this, that baby's health for its whole life depends upon you, girls, more than upon anything else." Simple rules, such as a girl of six could understand, are given for the feeding, washing, dressing, nursing, and even amusement of that important person, " baby."

And it is in her best known book of all that she says : " The healthiest, happiest, liveliest, most beautiful baby I ever saw was the only child of a busy laundress. She washed all day in a room with the door open upon a larger room, where she put the child. It sat or crawled upon the floor all day with no other playfellow than a kitten, which it used to hug. Its mother kept it beautifully clean, and fed it with perfect regularity. The child was never frightened at anything. The room where it sat was the house-place ; and it always gave notice to its mother when anybody came in, not by a cry, but by a crow. I lived for many months within hearing of that child, and never heard it cry day or night. I think there is a great deal too much

of amusing children now, and not enough of
letting them amuse themselves."

What, again, could be more useful in its simplicity than the following, addressed to working
mothers :—

"DEAR HARD-WORKING FRIENDS,—I am a
hard-working woman too. May I speak to
you ? And will you excuse me, though not a
mother ?

"You feel with me that every mother who
brings a child into the world has the duty laid
upon her of bringing up the child in such health
as will enable him to do the work of his life.

"But though you toil all day for your children,
and are so devoted to them, this is not at all an
easy task.

"We should not attempt to practise dress-
making, or any other trade, without any training
for it ; but it is generally impossible for a woman
to get any teaching about the management of
health ; yet health is to be learnt. . . .

"The cottage homes of England are, after all,
the most important of the homes of any class ;

they should be pure in every sense, pure in body and mind.

" Boys and girls must grow up healthy, with clean minds and clean bodies and clean skins.

" And for this to be possible, the air, the earth, and the water that they grow up in and have around them must be clean. Fresh air, not bad air ; clean earth, not foul earth ; pure water, not dirty water ; and the first teachings and impressions that they have at home must all be pure, and gentle, and firm. It is home that teaches the child, after all, more than any other schooling. A child learns before it is three whether it shall obey its mother or not ; and before it is seven, wise men tell us that its character is formed.

" There is, too, another thing—orderliness. We know your daily toil and love. May not the busiest and hardest life be somewhat lightened, the day mapped out, so that each duty has the same hours ? . . .

" Think what enormous extra trouble it entails on mothers when there is sickness. It is worth while to try to keep the family in health, to

Dec 16/96

10 SOUTH STREET,
PARK LANE W

Dear Duke of Westminster

Good speed to your noble effort in favour of District Nurses for town & "country"; and in commemoration of our Queen who cares for all, who look upon the District Nurse, if she is what she should be, &, if we give her the training she should have, as that great civilizer of the poor, training as well as nursing them out of ill health into good health (the little uncleanness), out of drink into self control but all without preaching, without

patronizing — as friends in sympathy.

But let them hold the standard high as Nurses

May be every little try to help all I can, tho' that be small, here & with your own care let you know.

Pray believe me
your Grace's faithful servant

Florence Nightingale

prevent the sorrow, the anxiety, the trouble of illness in the house, of which so much can be prevented.

"When a child has lost its health, how often the mother says, 'Oh, if I had only known! but there was no one to tell me.' And after all, it is health and not sickness that is our natural state—the state that God intends for us. There are more people to pick us up when we fall than to enable us to stand upon our feet. God did not intend all mothers to be accompanied by doctors, but He meant all children to be cared for by mothers. God bless your work and labour of love."

Or in a widely different field, in that fight against one of the most important causes of consumption, in which she was so far ahead of her time, what could be more clear and convincing, both in knowledge and in reasoning, than the following analysis with regard to army barracks :—

"The cavalry barracks, as a whole, are the least overcrowded, and have the freest external movement of air. Next come the infantry ; and the most crowded and the least ventilated externally are the Guards' barracks ; *so that the mortality from consumption, which follows the same order of increase in the different arms, augments with increase of crowding and difficulty of ventilation.*" *

Her own well-trained mind was in extreme contrast with the type of mind which she describes in the following story :—

" I remember, when a child, hearing the story of an accident, related by some one who sent two girls to fetch a 'bottle of sal volatile from her room.' 'Mary could not stir,' she said ; 'Fanny ran and fetched a bottle that was not sal volatile, and that was not in my room.' "

All her teaching, so far as I know it, is clearly at first-hand and carefully sifted. It is as far as possible from that useless kind of doctrine which is a mere echo of unthinking hearsay. For instance, how many sufferers she must have saved from unnecessary irritation by the following reminder to nurses :—

* The italics are added.

" Of all parts of the body, the face is perhaps the one which tells the least to the common observer or the casual visitor.

" I have known patients dying of sheer pain, exhaustion, and want of sleep, from one of the most lingering and painful diseases known, preserve, till within a few days of death, not only the healthy colour of the cheek, but the mottled appearance of a robust child. And scores of times have I heard these unfortunate creatures assailed with, ' I am glad to see you looking so well.' ' I see no reason why you should not live till ninety years of age.' ' Why don't you take a little more exercise and amusement ? '—with all the other commonplaces with which we are so familiar."

And then, again, how like her it is to remind those who are nursing that "a patient is not merely a piece of furniture, to be kept clean and arranged against the wall, and saved from injury or breakage."

She was one of the rare people who realized that truth of word is partly a question of education, and that many people are quite unconscious of their lack of that difficult virtue. "I know I fibbs dreadful," said a poor little servant girl to her once. "But believe me, miss, I never finds out I have fibbed until they tell me so!" And her comment suggests that in this matter that poor little servant girl by no means stood alone.

She worked very hard. Her books and pamphlets* were important, and her correspondence, ever dealing with the reforms she had at heart all over the world, was of itself an immense output.

Those who have had to write much from bed or sofa know only too well the abnormal fatigue it involves, and her labours of this kind seem to have been unlimited.

How strongly she sympathized with all municipal efforts, we see in many such letters as the one to General Evatt, given him for electioneering purposes, but not hitherto included in any biography, which we are allowed to reproduce here :—

* A complete list is subjoined in the Appendix.

"Strenuously desiring, as we all of us must, that *Administration* as well as Politics should be well represented in Parliament, and that vital matters of social, sanitary, and general interest should find their voice, we could desire no better representative and advocate of these essential matters—matters of life and death—than a man who, like yourself, unites with almost exhaustless energy and public spirit, sympathy with the wronged and enthusiasm with the right, a persevering acuteness in unravelling the causes of the evil and the good, large and varied experience and practical power, limited only by the nature of the object for which it is exerted.

"It is important beyond measure that such a man's thoughtful and well-considered opinions and energetic voice should be heard in the House of Commons.

"You have my warmest sympathy in your candidature for Woolwich, my best wishes that you should succeed, even less for your own sake than for that of Administration and of England.—Pray believe me, ever your faithful servant,

"FLORENCE NIGHTINGALE."

And also the following letter written to the Buckinghamshire County Council in 1892, begging them to appoint a sanitary committee :—

" We must create a public opinion which will drive the Government, instead of the Government having to drive us—an enlightened public opinion, wise in principles, wise in details. We hail the County Council as being or becoming one of the strongest engines in our favour, at once fathering and obeying the great impulse for national health against national and local disease. For we have learned that we have national health in our own hands—local sanitation, national health. But we have to contend against centuries of superstition and generations of indifference. Let the County Council take the lead."

And how justly, how clearly, she was able to weigh the work of those who had borne the brunt of sanitary inquiry in the Crimea, with but little except kicks for their pains, may be judged by the following sentences from a letter to Lady Tulloch in 1878 :—

"My Dear Lady Tulloch,—I give you joy, I give you both joy, for this crowning recognition of one of the noblest labours ever done on earth. You yourself cannot cling to it more than I do ; hardly so much, in one sense, for I saw how Sir John MacNeill's and Sir A. Tulloch's reporting was the salvation of the army in the Crimea. Without them everything that happened would have been considered ' all right.'

"Mr. Martin's note is perfect, for it does not look like an afterthought, nor as prompted by others, but as the flow of a generous and able man's own reflection, and careful search into authentic documents. Thank you again and again for sending it to me. It is the greatest consolation I could have had. Will you remember me gratefully to Mr. Paget, also to Dr. Balfour ? *I look back upon these twenty years as if they were yesterday, but also as if they were a thousand years.* Success be with us and the noble dead—and it has been success.—Yours ever,

"Florence Nightingale."

We see from this letter how warmly the

old memories dwelt with her, even while her hands were full of good work for the future.

The death of Lord Herbert in 1868 had been a blow that struck very deeply at her health and spirits.

In all her work of army reform she had looked up to him as her " Chief," hardly realizing, perhaps, how much of the initiating had been her own. Their friendship, too, had been almost life-long, and in every way ideal. The whole nation mourned his loss, but only the little intimate group which centred in his wife and children and those dearest friends, of whom Miss Nightingale was one, knew fully all that the country had lost in him.

It may be worth while for a double reason to quote here from Mr. Gladstone's tribute at a meeting held to decide on a memorial.

" To him," said Gladstone, "we owe the commission for inquiry into barracks and hospitals; to him we are indebted for the reorganization of the medical department of the army. To him

we owe the commission of inquiry into, and re-
modelling the medical education of, the army.
And, lastly, we owe him the commission for
presenting to the public the vital statistics of
the army in such a form, from time to time,
that the great and living facts of the subject are
brought to view."

Lord Herbert had toiled with ever-deepening
zeal to reform the unhealthy conditions to which,
even in times of peace, our soldiers had been
exposed—so unhealthy that, while the mortality
lists showed a death of eight in every thousand for
civilians, for soldiers the number of deaths was
seventeen per thousand. And of every two
deaths in the army it was asserted that one was
preventable. Lord Herbert was the heart and
soul of the Royal Commission to inquire into
these preventable causes, and through his working ardour the work branched forth into
four supplementary commissions concerning
hospitals and barracks. When he died, Miss
Nightingale not only felt the pang of parting
from one of her oldest and most valued friends, but

also felt that in this cause, so specially
to her heart, she had lost a helper who
d never be replaced, though she dauntlessly
l to her task and helped to carry on his
t.

CHAPTER XXI.

Multifarious work and many honours—Jubilee Nurses—Nursing Association—Death of father and mother—Lady Verney and her husband—No respecter of persons—From within four walls—South Africa and America.

HER activities were so multitudinous that it is difficult even to name them all in such a brief sketch as this. Besides those at which we have already glanced, prison reform, help to Bosnian fugitives, Manchester Police Court Mission for Lads, Indian Famine Fund—merely glancing down two pages of her biography, I find all these mentioned. She was herself, of course, decorated with the Red Cross, but M. Henri Dunant's magnificent Red Cross scheme for helping the wounded on the battlefield may be said to have been really the outcome of her own work and example. For it was the extension of her own activities, by means of the Red Cross

Societies, which throughout the European continent act in concert with their respective armies and governments.

She was the first woman to be decorated with the Order of Merit, which was bestowed on her in 1907, and in the following year she received, as the Baroness Burdett Coutts had done, the "Freedom of the City of London," having already been awarded, among many like honours, the French Gold Medal of Secours aux blessés Militaires, and the German Order of the Cross of Merit. On May 10, 1910, she received the badge of honour of the Norwegian Red Cross Society. But there was another distinction, even more unique, which was already hers. For when £70,000 came into Queen Victoria's hands as a gift from the women of her empire at the time of her Jubilee, so much had the Queen been impressed by the work of the Nursing Association and all that had been done for the sick poor, that the interest of this Women's Jubilee Fund, £2,000 a year, was devoted to an Institution for Training and Maintaining Nurses for the Sick Poor; and the National Association for Providing

Trained Nurses, which owed so much to Miss Nightingale, was affiliated with it, though it still keeps its old headquarters at 23 Bloomsbury Square, where for so many years would arrive at Christmas from her old home a consignment of beautiful holly and other evergreens for Christmas festivities. H.R.H. the Princess Christian is President of the Nursing Association, and Miss Nightingale's old friend and fellow-worker, Mr. Henry Bonham Carter, is the Secretary. The influence of Miss Florence Lees, described by Kinglake as "the gifted and radiant pupil of Florence Nightingale," who afterwards became Mrs. Dacre Craven, and was the first Superintendent-General, has been a very vitalizing influence there, and the home owes much also to her husband, the Rev. Dacre Craven, of St. Andrew's, Holborn. Miss Nightingale's warm friendship for Miss Florence Lees brought her into peculiarly intimate relations with the home, and both the Association and the Queen's Jubilee Institute are the fruit of Miss Nightingale's teaching, and a noble double memorial of the national—nay, imperial—recognition of its value.

The Royal Pension Fund for Nurses also, in which Queen Alexandra was so specially interested, helped to crown the fulfilment of Miss Nightingale's early dream and long, steadfast life-work.

But equally important, though less striking, has been the growing harvest of her quiet, courteous efforts to help village mothers to understand the laws of health, her pioneer-work in regard to all the dangers of careless milk-farms, her insistence on the importance of pure air as well as pure water, though she had always been careful to treat the poor man's rooftree as his castle and never to cross his doorstep except by permission or invitation.

After the death of her father at Embley in 1874—a very peaceful death, commemorated in the inscription on his tomb, "In Thy light we shall see light," which suggests in him a nature at once devout and sincere—she was much with her mother, in the old homes at Embley and Lea Hurst, though Lea Hurst was the one she loved best, and the beech-wood walk in Lea Woods, with its radiant shower of golden leaves in the autumn, for which she would sometimes delay her leaving, is still specially associated with her memory: and her thoughtfulness for the poor still expressed itself in many different ways —in careful gifts, for instance, through one whom she trusted for knowledge and tact; in her arrangement that pure milk should be sent daily from the home dairy at Lea Hurst to those in need of it.

With faithful love she tended her mother to the time of her death in 1880, and there seems to be a joyous thanksgiving for that mother's beauty of character in the words the two sisters inscribed to her memory: "God is love—Bless the Lord, O my soul, and forget not all His benefits."

After her mother's death, when the property had passed into the hands of Mr. William Shore Nightingale, she still visited her kinsman there and kept up her interest in the people of the district.

Among the outward events of her life, after her return from the Crimea, one of the earliest had been the marriage of her sister Parthenope,

who in 1858 became the second wife of Sir
Harry Verney,* and her home at Claydon in
Buckinghamshire was thenceforth a second home
to Miss Nightingale. It need hardly be said
that in Sir Harry Verney's various generous
schemes for the good of the neighbourhood,
schemes in which his wife cordially co-operated,
Miss Nightingale took a warm and sympathetic
pleasure. His keen interest in army reform was,
of course, a special ground of comradeship.
Miss Nightingale divided her time chiefly between her own home in South Street, Park Lane,
and visits to the rooms that were reserved for
her at Claydon. One of her great interests
while at Claydon, soon after her sister's marriage,
had been the building of the new Buckinghamshire Infirmary in 1861, of which her sister laid
the foundation; and her bust still adorns the
entrance hall.

Mrs. Tooley reminds us that not only was
Lady Verney well known in literary and political
circles, but also her books on social questions

* Sir Harry Verney died four years later, and Claydon then
passed to Sir Edmund Hope Verney, the son of his first marriage.

had the distinction of being quoted in the House of Commons. She gives many interesting details with regard to the philanthropic and political work of Sir Harry Verney and his family, but it is hardly necessary to duplicate them here, since her book is still available. Lady Verney's death in 1890, after a long and painful illness, following on that of her father and mother, bereaved Miss Nightingale of a lifelong companionship, and might have left her very lonely but for her absorbing work and her troops of friends.

How fruitful that work was we may dimly see when we remember that—to instance one branch of it only—in ten years the death-rate in the army in India, which her efforts so determinately strove to lessen, fell from sixty-nine per thousand to eighteen per thousand.* She strove—and not in vain—to improve the sanitary conditions of immense areas of undrained country, but she also endeavoured to bring home to the rank and file of the army individual teaching.

She gives in one of her pamphlets a delightful story of men who came to a district in India

* " Life of Florence Nightingale," by Sarah Tooley, p. 295.

supposed to be fatal to any new-comer, but, strong in their new hygienic knowledge, determined *not* to have cholera. They lived carefully, they grew their own garden produce, they did not give way to fear, and *all*, without exception, escaped.

To return for a moment to Britain, since a separate chapter is reserved for India. She was before her day in contending that foul air was one of the great causes of consumption and other diseases. And her teaching was ever given with courtesy and consideration. How strongly she felt on this and kindred subjects, and how practical her help was, we see clearly in her letters and pamphlets. She delighted in making festivities for companies of nurses and of her other hard-working friends. And in St. Paul's fine sense of the phrase, she was no " respecter of persons": she reverenced personality, not accidental rank. She had no patience with those visiting ladies who think they may intrude at all hours of the day into the homes of the poor, and her quick sense of humour delighted in many of the odd speeches which would have shocked the prim and conventional. She thought the highest compliment ever paid to her staff of nurses who visited in the homes of the poor was the speech of the grubby ragamuffin, who seemed to think they could wash off even the blackness of the Arch-fiend and, when being scrubbed, cried out, " You may bathe the divil."

But with all her fun and relish of life, how sane, how practical, she was !

Do you remember how she laughed at the silly idea that nothing was needed to make a good nurse except what the " Early Victorian " used to call " a disappointment in love " ?

Here are other of her shrewd sayings from her *Nursing Notes* :—

" Another extraordinary fallacy is the dread of night air. What air can we breathe at night but night air ? The choice is between pure night air from without and foul air from within. Most people prefer the latter. . . . Without cleanliness within and without your house, ventilation is comparatively useless. . . . And now, you think these things trifles, or at least exaggerated. But what you ' think ' or what I 'think' matters little. Let us see what God thinks of them. God always justifies His ways. While we are thinking, He has been teaching. I have known cases of hospital pyæmia quite as severe in handsome private houses as in any of the worst hospitals, and from the same cause—viz., foul air. Yet nobody learnt the lesson. Nobody learnt *anything* at all from it. They went on *thinking*—thinking that the sufferer had scratched his thumb, or that it was singular that 'all the servants' had 'whitlows,' or that something was 'much about this year.'"

If there had been any hope at first that Miss Nightingale might grow strong enough to stand visibly among those who were being trained as nurses by the fund raised in her honour, that hope was now past, and when the great new wing of St. Thomas's was built—the finest building for its purpose in Europe—the outward reins of government had to be delivered over into the hands of another, though hers was throughout the directing hand. And the results of her work are written in big type upon the page of history.

In India and America she is acclaimed as an adored benefactress, but what has she not done for our own country alone? To sum up even a few of the points on which I have touched: she initiated sick nursing among the poor, through her special appeal was built the Central Home for Nurses, she was the pioneer in the hygienic work of county councils, and, besides the great nursing school at St. Thomas's, to her was largely due the reform of nursing in workhouses and infirmaries. And in 1890, with the £70,000 of the Women's Jubilee Fund, the establishment of the Queen's Nurses received its charter.

In affairs of military nursing it is no exaggeration to say that she was consulted throughout the world. America came to her in the Civil War; South Africa owed much to her; India infinitely more; and so vital have been the reforms introduced by Lord Herbert and herself that even as early as 1880, when General Gordon was waging war in China during the Taiping Rebellion, the death-rate as compared with the Crimea was reduced from sixty per cent. to little more than three in every hundred yearly.*

We have seen that, though she was so much more seriously broken in health than any one at first realized, that did not prevent her incessant work, though it did in the end make her life more or less a hidden life, spent within four walls, and chiefly on her bed.

Yet from those four walls what electric messages of help and common sense were continuously flashing across the length and breadth of the world! She was regarded as an expert in her own subjects, and long before her Jubilee Fund enabled her to send forth the Queen's Nurses, she was, as we have already seen, busy writing and working to improve not only nursing in general, but especially the nursing of the sick poor ; and unceasingly she still laboured for the army.

Repeated mention has been made of General Evatt, to whose memory of Miss Nightingale I am much indebted.

General Evatt served in the last Afghan

* See "Life of Florence Nightingale," by Sarah Tooley, p. 268.

campaign, and what he there experienced determined him to seek an interview, as soon as
he returned to England, with her whom he
regarded as the great reformer of military hygiene
—Florence Nightingale. In this way and on
this subject there arose between them a delightful and enduring friendship. Many and many a
time in that quiet room in South Street where
she lay upon her bed—its dainty coverlet all
strewn with the letters and papers that might
have befitted the desk or office of a busy states-
man, and surrounded by books and by the flowers
that she loved so well—he had talked with her
for four hours on end, admiring with a sort
of wonder her great staying power and her
big, untiring brain.

He did not, like another acquaintance of mine,
say that he came away feeling like a sucked
orange, with all hoarded knowledge on matters
great and small gently, resistlessly drawn from
him by his charming companion; but so voracious was the eager, sympathetic interest of Miss
Nightingale in the men and women of that active
world whose streets, at the time he learned to

know her, she no longer walked, that no conversation on human affairs ever seemed, he said,
to tire her.

And her mind was ever working towards new
measures for the health and uplifting of her
fellow-creatures.

We have seen how eager she was to use for
good every municipal opportunity, but she did
not stop at the municipality, for she knew that
there are many womanly. duties also at the
imperial hearth ; and without entering on any
controversy, it is necessary to state clearly that
she very early declared herself in favour of
household suffrage for women, and that " the
North of England Society for Women's Suffrage
is the proud possessor of her signature to an
address to Mr. Disraeli, thanking him for his
favourable vote in the House of Commons, and
begging him to do his utmost to remove the
injustice under which women householders
suffered by being deprived of the parliamentary
vote." *

* " Florence Nightingale," a Cameo Life-Sketch by Marion
Holmes.

Florence Nightingale's London House, 10 South Street,
Park Lane (house with balcony), where she died,
August 14, 1910.

Whatever could aid womanly service—as a voice in choosing our great domestic executive nowadays undoubtedly can—had her sympathy and interest ; but what she emphasized most, I take it, at all times, was that when any door opened for service, woman should be not only willing, but also nobly *efficient*. She herself opened many such doors, and her lamp was always trimmed and filled and ready to give light and comfort in the darkest room.

It has been well said that in describing a friend in the following words, she unconsciously drew a picture of herself :—

"She had the gracefulness, the wit, the unfailing cheerfulness—qualities so remarkable, but so much overlooked, in our Saviour's life. She had the absence of all 'mortification' for mortification's sake, which characterized His work, and any real work in the present day as in His day. And how did she do all this ? . . . She was always filled with the thought that she must be about her Father's business."

CHAPTER XXII.

India—Correspondence with Sir Bartle Frere—Interest in village girls—The Lamp.

WE come now to Miss Nightingale's most monumental achievement of all, the reform of sanitary conditions in India—a reform ever widening and developing, branching forth and striking its roots deeper. Her interest in that vast population, that world-old treasury of subtle religious thought and ever-present mystical faith, may perhaps have been in part an inheritance from the Anglo-Indian Governor who was counted in her near ancestry. But there can be little doubt that her ardent and practical desire to improve the conditions of camp life in India began in her intimate care for the soldiers, and her close knowledge of many things unknown to the ordinary English subject. The world-wide freemasonry of the rank and file in

our army enabled her to hear while at Scutari
much of the life of the army in the vast and
distant dominions of Burma and Bengal, and
she had that gift for seeing through things to
their farthest roots which enabled her to perceive
clearly that no mere mending of camp conditions
could stay the continual ravages of disease among
our men. The evil was deeper and wider, and
only as conditions were improved in sanitary matters could the mortality of the army be lessened.
She saw, and saw clearly, that the reason children died like flies in India, so that those who
loved them best chose the agony of years of parting rather than take the risks, lay not so much
in the climate as in the human poisons and
putrefactions so carelessly treated and so quickly
raised to murder-power by the extreme heat.

Much of this comes out clearly in her letter
to Sir Bartle Frere, with whom her first ground
of friendship had arisen out of their common
interest in sanitary matters.

What manner of man Sir Bartle was may be
divined from a letter to him written by Colonel
W. F. Marriott, one of the secretaries of the

Bombay Government, at the time of his leaving Bombay :—

"The scene of your departure stirred me much. That bright evening, the crowd on the pier and shore as the boat put off, the music from the *Octavia*, as the band played 'Auld Lang Syne' as we passed, were all typical and impressive by association of ideas. But it was not a shallow sympathy with which I took in all the circumstances. I could divine some of your thoughts. If I felt like Sir Bedivere, left behind 'among new men, strange faces, other minds,' you must have felt in some degree like King Arthur in the barge, 'I have lived my life, and that which I have done may He Himself make pure.' I do not doubt that you felt that all this 'mouth honour' is only worth so far as it is the seal of one's own approving conscience, and though you could accept it freely as deserved from their lips, yet at that hour you judged your own work hardly. You measured the palpable results with your conceptions and hopes, and were inclined to say, 'I am no better

than my fathers.' But I, judging now calmly
and critically, feel—I may say, see—that though
the things that seem to have failed be amongst
those for which you have taken most pains, yet
they are small things compared with the work
which has not failed. You have made an
impression of earnest human sympathy with the
people of this country, which will deepen and
expand, so that it will be felt as a perpetual
witness against any narrower and less noble
conception of our relation to them, permanently
raising the moral standard of highest policy
towards them ; and your name will become a
traditional embodiment of a good governor." *

Frere had seen that the filthy condition of
many of the roads, after the passing of animals
and the failure to cleanse from manure, was of
itself a source of poison, though the relation between garbage and disease-bearing flies was then
less commonly understood, and he was never tired
of urging the making of decent roads ; but this,

* "Life of Sir Bartle Frere," by John Martineau. (John
Murray.)

he knew, was only a very small part of the improvements needed.

His correspondence with Miss Nightingale began in 1867, and in that and the five following years they exchanged about one hundred letters, chiefly on sanitary questions.

It was part of her genius always to see and seize her opportunity, and she rightly thought that, as she says in one of her letters, "We might never have such a favourable conjunction of the larger planets again :

"You, who are willing and most able to organize the machinery here ; Sir John Lawrence, who is able and willing, provided only he knew what to do ; and a Secretary of State who is willing and in earnest. And I believe nothing would bring them to their senses in India more than an annual report of what they have done, with your comments upon it, laid before Parliament."

In order to set in motion the machinery of a sanitary department for all India, a despatch had to be written, pointing out clearly and concisely what was to be done.

Frere consulted Miss Nightingale at every

point about this despatch, but spoke of the
necessity for some sort of peg to hang it on
—"not," he said, "that the Secretary of State is
at all lukewarm, nor, I think, that he has any
doubt as to what should be said, or how—that,
I think, your memoranda have fixed ; the only
difficulty is as to the when. . . .

"No governor-general, I believe, since the
time of Clive has had such powers and such
opportunities, but he fancies the want of progress
is owing to some opposing power which does
not exist anywhere but in his own imagination.

"He cannot see that perpetual inspection by
the admiral of the drill and kit of every sailor is
not the way to make the fleet efficient, and he
gets disheartened and depressed because he finds
that months and years of this squirrel-like activity
lead to no real progress."

The despatch with its accompanying documents
went to Miss Nightingale for her remarks before it
was sent out. Her commentary was as follows :—

"I find nothing to add or to take away in the
memorandum (sanitary). It appears to me quite

perfect in itself—that is, it is quite as much as the enemy will bear, meaning by the enemy—not at all the Government of India in India, still less the Government of India at home, but —that careless and ignorant person called the Devil, who is always walking about taking knowledge out of people's heads, who said that he was coming to give us the knowledge of good and evil, and who has done just the contrary.

"It is a noble paper, an admirable paper—and what a present to make to a government! You have included in it all the great principles —sanitary and administrative—which the country requires. And now you must work, work these points until they are embodied in local works in India. This will not be in our time, for it takes more than a few years to fill a continent with civilization. But I never despair that in God's good time every man of us will reap the common benefit of obeying all the laws which He has given us for our well-being.

"I shall give myself the pleasure of writing to you again about these papers. But I write this

Florence Nightingale in her Last Days.

(From a drawing from memory.   Copyright A. Rischgitz.)

note merely to say that I don't think this memorandum requires any addition.

" God bless you for it ! I think it is a great work."*

It *was* a great work, and it might have been delayed for scores of years, with a yearly unnecessary waste of thousands of lives, if she had not initiated it.

Her words to Sir Bartle Frere at the outset had been : " It does seem that there is no element in the scheme of government (of India) by which the public health can be taken care of. And the thing is now to create such an element."

As early as 1863, in her " Observations on the Sanitary State of the Army in India," she had written :—

" Native ' caste ' prejudices appear to have been made the excuse for European laziness, as far as regards our sanitary and hospital neglects of the natives. Recent railroad experience is a striking proof that ' caste,' in their minds, is

* "Life of Sir Bartle Frere," by John Martineau. (John Murray.)

no bar to intercommunication in arrangements tending to their benefit."

Sir C. Trevelyan justly says that "a good sanitary state of the military force cannot be secured without making similar arrangements for the populations settled in and around the military cantonments; that sanitary reform must be generally introduced into India for the civil as well as the military portion of the community."

And now that the opportunity arrived, all was done with wise and swift diplomacy. The way was smoothed by a call from Frere on his old friend Sir Richard Temple, at that time Finance Minister at Calcutta, asking him to help.

Those who know India best, and know Miss Nightingale best, are those who are most aware of the mighty tree of ever-widening health improvement that grew from this little seed, and of the care with which Miss Nightingale helped to guard and foster it.

"She was a great Indian," her friend General Evatt repeated to me more than once, "and what a head she had! She was the only human being I have ever met, for instance, man or woman, who had thoroughly mastered the intricate details of the Bengal land-purchase system. She loved India, and she knew it through and through. It was no wonder that every distinguished Indian who came to England went to see Miss Nightingale."

She bore her ninety years very lightly, and made a vision serene and noble, as will be seen from our picture, though that does not give the lovely youthful colouring in contrast with the silvery hair, and we read of the great expressiveness of her hands, which, a little more, perhaps, than is usual with Englishwomen, she used in conversation.

It was a very secluded life that she lived at No. 10 South Street; but she was by no means without devotees, and the bouquet that the German Emperor sent her was but one of many offerings from many high-hearted warriors at her shrine.

And when she visited her old haunts at Lea Hurst and Embley she delighted in sending invitations to the girls growing up in those village families that she had long counted among her friends, so that to her tea-table were lovingly welcomed guests very lowly, as well as those better known to the world.

Her intense and sympathetic interest in all the preparations for nursing in the South African campaign has already been touched upon, as well as her joy that some of her own nurses from among the first probationers at St. Thomas's were accepted in that enterprise with praise and gratitude.

It would be a serious omission not to refer my readers to a very moving letter which she wrote to Cavaliere Sebastiano Fenzi, during the Italian War of Independence in 1866, of which a part is given in Mrs. Tooley's book, and from which I am permitted to quote the following:—

"I have given dry advice as dryly as I could. But you must permit me to say that if there is anything I could do for you at any time, and you would command me, I should esteem it the greatest honour and pleasure. I am a hopeless invalid, entirely a prisoner to my room, and overwhelmed with business.   Otherwise how gladly would I answer to your call and come and do my little best for you in the dear city where I was born.   If the giving my miserable life could hasten your success but by half an hour, how gladly would I give it !"

How far she was ahead of her time becomes every day more obvious ; for every day the results of her teaching are gradually making themselves felt.   For example, it can no longer, without qualification, be said, as she so truly said in her own day, that while " the coxcombries of education are taught to every schoolgirl " there is gross ignorance, not only among schoolgirls, but also even among mothers and nurses, with regard to " those laws which God has assigned to the relations of our bodies with the world in which He has put them.   In other words, the laws which make these bodies, into which He has put our minds, healthy or unhealthy organs of those minds, are all but unlearnt.   Not but that these laws—the laws of life—are in a certain measure understood, but not even mothers think

it worth their while to study them—to study
how to give their children healthy existences.
They call it medical or physiological knowledge,
fit only for doctors."

In her old age, loved and honoured far and
wide, she toiled on with all the warm enthusiasm
of a girl, and the ripe wisdom of fourscore
years and ten spent in the service of her one
Master, for she was not of those who ever
tried to serve two. And when she died at
No. 10 South Street, on August 10, 1910—
died so peacefully that the tranquil glow of
sunset descended upon her day of harvest—the
following beautiful incident was recorded in
Nursing Notes, to whose editor I am specially
indebted for bringing to my notice the verses in
which the story is told * :—

> " At Chelsea, under the lime tree's stir,
>   I read the news to a pensioner
>   That a noble lord and a judge were dead—
>   ' They were younger men than me,' he said.

> " I read again of another death ;
>   The old man turned, and caught his breath—

---

* " The Lady of the Lamp," by F. S., reprinted from the *Evening
News* of August 16, 1910, in *Nursing Notes* of September 1, 1910.

'She's gone?' he said; 'she too? In camp
We called her the Lady of the Lamp.'

" He would not listen to what I read,
But wanted it certain—'The Lady's dead?'
I showed it him to remove his doubt,
And added, unthinking, 'The Lamp is out.'

" He rose—and I had to help him stand—
Then, as he saluted with trembling hand,
I was abashed to hear him say,
'The Lamp she lit is alight to-day.'"

F. S.

CHAPTER XXIII.

A brief summing up.

THOSE who write of Florence Nightingale sentimentally, as though she spent herself in a blind, caressing tenderness, would have earned her secret scorn, not unflavoured by a jest; for she stood always at the opposite pole from the sentimentalists, and perhaps had a little of her father in her—that father who, when he was *giving* right and left, would say to some plausible beggar of society who came to him for wholesale subscriptions, "You see, I was not born generous," well knowing that his ideas of generosity and theirs differed by a whole heaven, and that his were the wider and the more generous of the two.

She had a will of iron. That is what one of her greatest admirers has more than once said to me—and he knew her well. No doubt it was

true. Only a will of iron could have enabled
a delicate woman to serve, for twenty hours
at a time, with unwearying tenderness and
courage among the wounded and the dying.
Even her iron resolution and absolute fearlessness
could not prevent her from taking Crimean fever
when she insisted on visiting a second time
the lonely typhus patient outside Balaclava, at
a moment when she was worn out with six
months of nursing and administration combined.
But it did enable her to go back to her post
when barely recovered, and, later in life, even
when a prisoner within four walls, who seldom
left her bed, that will of iron did enable her
to go on labouring till the age of ninety, and
to fulfil for the good of mankind the dearest
purpose of her heart. Nothing is harder than
iron, and that which is made of it after it has
been through the furnace has long been the very
symbol of loyalty and uprightness when we
say of a man that he is " true as steel."

Yes, iron is hard and makes a pillar of strength
in time of need. But he who forges out of
it weapons and tools that are at once delicate

and resistless, knows that it will humbly shoe the feet of horses, and cut the household bread, and will make for others besides Lombardy a kingly crown. And when iron is truly on fire, nothing commoner or softer nor anything more yielding—not even gold itself—can glow with a more steadfast and fervent heat to warm the hands and hearts of men.

The picture of Miss Nightingale that dwells in the popular mind no doubt owes its outline to the memories of the men she nursed with such tenderness and skill. And it is a true picture. Like all good workmen, she loved her work, and nursing was her chosen work so long as her strength remained. None can read her writing, and especially her *Nursing Notes* and her pamphlet on nursing among the sick poor, without feeling how much she cared for every minutest detail, and how sensitively she felt with, and for, her patients.

But such a picture, as will have been made clear by this time, shows only one aspect of her life-work. One of her nearest intimates writes to me of her difficulties in reforming military hospitals, and her determination therefore to give herself later in life to the reform of civilian nursing ; but in reality she did both, for through the one she indirectly influenced the other, and began what has been widening and unfolding in every direction ever since.

Those who knew her best speak almost with awe of her constructive and organizing power. She was indeed a pioneer and a leader, and girt about with the modesty of all true greatness.

Like Joan of Arc, she heeded not the outward voices, but, through all faults and sorrows, sought to follow always and only the voice of the Divine One. This gave her life unity and power. And when she passed on into the life beyond, the door opened and closed again very quietly, leaving the whole world the better for her ninety years in our midst. " When I have done with this old suit," says George Meredith, " so much in need of mending ; " but hers, like his, was a very charming suit to the last, and even to the end of her ninety years the colouring was clear and fresh as a girl's.

Like all strong, true, disinterested people, she

made enemies—where is there any sanitary reformer who does not?—yet seldom indeed has
any one, man or woman, won deeper and more
world-wide love.   But that was not her aim ;
her aim was to do the will of her Commander
and leave the world better than she found it.

Seldom has there been a moment when
women have more needed the counsel given
in one of the letters here published for the first
time, when she begs of a dear friend that her
name may be that " of one who obeys authority,
however unreasonable, in the name of Him who
is above all, and who is Reason itself."

And as we think of the debt the world owes
to Florence Nightingale and of all she did for
England, for India, and not only for the British
Empire, but for the world, we may well pause
for a moment on the words that closed our
opening chapter, in which she begs her fellow-
workers to give up considering their actions
in any light of rivalry as between men and
women, and ends with an entreaty :—

" It does not make a thing good, that it

is remarkable that a woman should have been
able to do it. Neither does it make a thing
bad, which would have been good had a man
done it, that it has been done by a woman.

"Oh, leave these jargons, and go your way
straight to God's work, in simplicity and singleness of heart."

The well-remembered words of Ruskin's appeal to girls in "Sesame and Lilies," published
but a few years earlier, were evidently in Miss
Nightingale's mind when she wrote the closing
sentences of her tribute to Agnes Jones —
sentences which set their seal upon this volume,
and will echo long after it is forgotten.

"Let us," she writes, "add living flowers to
her grave, 'lilies with full hands,' not fleeting
primroses, nor dying flowers. Let us bring the
work of our hands and our heads and our hearts
to finish her work which God has so blessed.
Let us not merely rest in peace, but let hers be
the life which stirs up to fight the good fight
against vice and sin and misery and wretchedness,

as she did—the call to arms which she was ever obeying :—

> ' The Son of God goes forth to war—
> Who follows in His train ? '

"O daughters of God, are there so few to answer ? "

APPENDIX.

LIST OF PUBLICATIONS BY FLORENCE NIGHTINGALE.

Letter (on the Madras Famine) : The Great Lesson of the Indian Famine, etc. 1877.

Life or Death in India. A Paper read at the Meeting of the National Association for the Promotion of Social Science, Norwich, 1873, with an Appendix on Life or Death by Irrigation. 1874.

Notes on Hospitals : being two Papers read before the National Association for the Promotion of Science . . . 1858, with the evidence given to the Royal Commissioners on the state of the Army in 1857 (Appendix, Sites and Construction of Hospitals, etc.).

Do., 3rd Edition, enlarged, and for the most part rewritten. 1863.

Notes on Matters affecting the Health, Efficiency, and Hospital Administration of the British Army, founded chiefly on the experience of the late war. 1858.

Notes on Nursing : What it is, and what it is not. 1860.

New Edition, revised and enlarged, 1860 ; another Edition, 1876.

Miss Florence Nightingale ovy knitra o ošctřování nemocných. z anglického přeložila. Králova, 1872.

Des Soins a donner aux malades ce qu'il faut faire, ce qu'il faut eviter. Ouvrage traduit de l'Anglais. 1862.

Notes on Nursing for the Labouring Classes, with a Chapter on Children. 1861.

Do., New Edition, 1868 and 1876.

Observations on the . . . Sanitary State of the Army in India. Reprinted from the Report of the Royal Commission. 1863.

On Trained Nursing for the Sick Poor . . . A Letter . . . to *The Times* . . . April 14, 1876.

Sanitary Statistics of Native Nursing Schools and Hospitals. 1863.

Reproduction of a printed Report originally submitted to the Bucks County Council in the year 1892, containing Letters from Miss Florence Nightingale on Health Visiting in Rural Districts. 1911.

Statements exhibiting the Voluntary Contributions received by Miss Nightingale for the Use of the British War Hospitals in the East, with the mode of their Distribution in 1854, 1855, 1856. Published, London, 1857.

A LIST OF SOME OF THE BOOKS CONSULTED

In case any of my readers wish to read further for themselves :—

Kinglake's *Invasion of the Crimea.* (William Blackwood.)

Memoir of Sidney Herbert, by Lord Stanmore. (John Murray.)

Life of Sir Bartle Frere, by John Martineau. (John Murray.)

Letters of John Stuart Mill, edited by John Elliot. (Longmans.)

William Rathbone, a Memoir by Eleanor F. Rathbone. (Macmillan.)

The Life of Florence Nightingale, by Sarah Tooley. (Cassell.)

Felicia Skene of Oxford, by E. C. Rickards. (John Murray.)

Memoir of Sir John MacNeill, G.C.B., by his Granddaughter. (John Murray.)

Agnes Elizabeth Jones, by her Sister. (Alexander Strahan.)

A History of Nursing, by M. Adelaide Nutting, R.N., and Lavinia L. Dock, R.N. (G. P. Putnam and Sons.)

A Sister of Mercy's Memories of the Crimea, by Sister Aloysius. (Burns and Oates.)

The Story of Florence Nightingale, by W. I. W. (Pilgrim Press.)

Soyer's Culinary Campaign, by Alexis Soyer. (Routledge.)

Kaiserswerth, by Florence Nightingale.

Florence Nightingale, a Cameo Life-Sketch by Marion Holmes. (Women's Freedom League.)

Paterson's Roads, edited by Edward Mogg. (Longmans, Green, Orme.)

The London Library, No. 3, vol. of *The Times* for 1910.

Nursing Notes, by Florence Nightingale, and other writings of Miss Nightingale included in the foregoing list.

A BRIEF SKETCH
OF GENERAL EVATT'S CAREER.

[As given in *Who's Who*.]

EVATT, SURGEON-GENERAL GEORGE JOSEPH HAMILTON, C.B., 1903; M.D., R.A.M.C.; retired; Member, Council British Medical Association, 1904; born, 11th Nov. 1843; son of Captain George Evatt, 70th Foot; married, 1877, Sophie Mary Frances, daughter of William Walter Raleigh Kerr, Treasurer of Mauritius, and granddaughter of Lord Robert Kerr; one son, one daughter. Educated, Royal College of Surgeons, and Trinity College, Dublin. Entered Army Medical Service, 1865; joined 25th (K.O.S.B.) Regiment, 1866; Surgeon-Major, 1877; Lieutenant-Colonel, R.A.M.C., 1885; Colonel, 1896; Surgeon-General, 1899; served Perak Expedition with Sir H. Ross's Bengal

Column, 1876 (medal and clasp) ; Afghan War,
1878–80 ; capture of Ali Musjid (despatches) ;
action in Bazaar Valley, with General Tytler's
Column (despatches) ; advance on Gundamak,
and return in " Death March," 1879 (specially
thanked in General Orders by Viceroy of India
in Council and Commander-in-Chief in India
for services) ; commanded Field Hospital in
second campaign, including advance to relief
of Cabul under General Sir Charles Gough,
1879 ; action on the Ghuzni Road ; return to
India, 1880 (medal and two clasps) ; Suakin
Expedition, 1885, including actions at Handoub,
Tamai, and removal of wounded from MacNeill's
zareba (despatches, medal and clasp, Khedive's
Star) ; Zhob Valley Expedition, 1890 ; commanded a Field Hospital (despatches) ; Medical
Officer, Royal Military Academy, Woolwich,
1880–96 ; Senior Medical Officer, Quetta
Garrison, Baluchistan, 1887–91 ; Sanitary Officer,
Woolwich Garrison, 1892–94 ; Secretary, Royal
Victoria Hospital, Netley, 1894–96 ; P.M.O.,
China, 1896–99 ; P.M.O., Western District,
1899–1902 ; Surgeon-General, 2nd Army Corps,

Salisbury, 1902–3; raised with Mr. Cantlie R.A.M.C. Volunteers, 1883; founded, 1884, Medical Officers. of Schools Association, London; and, 1886, drew up scheme for Army Nursing Service Reserve; Member, Committee International Health Exhibition, 1884; Member of Council, Royal Army Temperance Association, 1903; President, Poor Law Medical Officers' Association; contested (L.) Woolwich, 1886, Fareham Division, Hampshire, 1906, and Brighton, 1910; Honorary Colonel, Home Counties Division, R.A.M.C., Territorial Force, 1908; received Distinguished Service Reward, 1910. *Publications:* Travels in the Euphrates Valley and Mesopotamia, 1873; and many publications on military and medical subjects.

THE END.

Printed in Great Britain
by Amazon

19858236R00233